HELP YOURSELF
to HAPPINESS

One Attitude At A Time

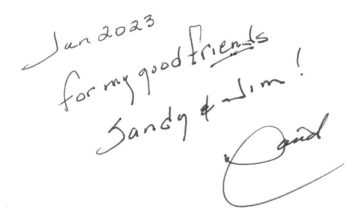

Jan 2023
for my good friends
Sandy & Jim !
David

DAVID A. BROWN, PH.D.

Printed in the United States of America.

Library of Congress Control Number: 2022943569

ISBN   Paperback   978-1-68536-757-2
              eBook   978-1-68536-758-9

Westwood Books Publishing LLC
Atlanta Financial Center
3343 Peachtree Rd NE Ste 145-725
Atlanta, GA 30326

www.westwoodbookspublishing.com

Help Yourself to Happiness: One Attitude at a Time

"Dr. David Brown's book has been used at Hodges University for many years and it has had a positive impact on everyone who has read it. Its aphorisms, vignettes and longer segments focus on challenging everyday occurrences and shed light on how perceptions and beliefs often color reactions to these situations. "Food for Thought" calls upon readers to reflect on their own life after they have read a piece. The questions are so compelling that readers often cannot resist the urge to respond. Through it all the message is that we can choose how we approach each situation.

Dr. Brown insists that we can control how we feel by the thoughts we have. One of my favorites is "The Death Call" in which he asks why a husband would smile after receiving a message that his wife has died. Once he explains that the husband was remembering many enjoyable and tender moments spent with his wife, the point is made - "The choice of which thoughts and feelings is up to me [you]." Such stories and others like "Yes I Can", "Fake it … Till You Make It!" and "Stinky" have become instructor favorites because of the impact they have had on students.

Students who have used the text say of it, "It taught me that I could succeed." "It made me look at myself differently"; "I felt that Dr. Brown was speaking directly to me through some of the readings"; "I gave up bad habits after reading the book." It has been so powerful a text that oftentimes students will purchase copies for friends and family members."

Dr. Elsa Rogers
Dean, School of Liberal Arts
Hodges University, Fort Myers

iii

Help Yourself to Happiness: One Attitude at a Time

"Here's the chance to have the Psych course you always wanted, and also really needed. Using stories ever so gracefully, Brown weaves theory and reality into memorable pages with genuine impact. The book is wise, insightful, even enthralling, and above all, REAL."

Sidney B. Simon, Professor Emeritus
Psychological Education
University of Massachusetts, Amherst

Help Yourself to Happiness: One Attitude at a Time

"Very practical and straightforward … this book can change lives! If it were required reading in schools…maybe we'd see more smiles and less crime on the streets."

Maryann Morley, RN
Asheville, NC

Help Yourself to Happiness: One Attitude at a Time

"Positive impact in my life! Dr. Brown's insights are a wonderful shift in the field of psychology from one of diagnosis of illness to actual change of action. I have used his suggestions in my life and am reaping rich rewards. Why to go, Doc!"

Donna W. Draw, Student
Communications Major, Hodges University

Help Yourself to Happiness: One Attitude at a Time

"Reading *Help Yourself to Happiness: One Attitude at a Time* was very useful to me. It is welcoming and helpful, valuable, realistic, and straight-forward. I am grateful for the opportunity to have read this book and I am inspired to change. You're pretty awesome, Doc!"

Charline Desrameaux, Student
Paralegal Studies, Hodges University

Help Yourself to Happiness: One Attitude at a Time

"Help Yourself to Happiness: One Attitude at a Time is a wonderful book. Dr. Brown's wisdom and knowledge helped me with my situation and to change my life. I really enjoyed reading "Puppets;" we are in charge of what we think and feel. I even use Dr. Brown's words when I am talking to my own children and informing them that they are in control of their lives.

It is enjoyable and useful. One of the better books that I have read. Thank you, Dr. Brown for changing my life."

George Powell, Student
Psychology Major, Hodges University

Help Yourself to Happiness: One Attitude at a Time

I had the pleasure of reading David A. Brown's current work within the arena of cognitive-behavioral change. When Dr. Brown originally launched The Pocket Therapist, I had the pleasure of witnessing it from the Front Row, as I was then a junior colleague of his at a community mental health center. Consequently, I am familiar with a number of the anecdotes he has included in this most recent iteration, and I am especially pleased to witness the creativity displayed through his use of pertinent points of emphasis which, in turn, are the subject of his and his students' contemplation and discussion. It is through this approach that he portrays the give-and-take that often occurs within the therapeutic alliance, and thereby extends the benefit beyond the 1:1 therapist-patient encounter. This captures the essence of Allport's request of us that we find meaningful ways in which we "give psychology away." In this work I believe that Dr. Brown has not only followed this dictum, but has also been able to share an integral part of himself; that of the insightful, warm, and thought-provoking teacher and therapist that I've known him to be for the past 30 years. This book most artfully strikes a unique balance as easy-to-read on the one hand while, on the other, maintaining its ability to serve as a catalyst of the reader's efforts at self-contemplation and personal growth. I very much enjoyed it, and am confident that you will as well.

Duane F. Hurst, Ph.D., Counseling Psychologist
Scottsdale, Arizona

ACKNOWLEDGEMENTS

Many special thanks to the rational educators in my life who have meant
so very much to me . . .

To

George E. Axtelle
Dorothy H. Brown
Lawrence E. Brown
Marcia C. Brown
Albert Ellis
Viktor E. Frankl
Duane F. Hurst
Maxie C. Maultsby, Jr.
Abraham H. Maslow
Walter S. Nosal
David N. Ruth
Sid Simon
William D. Wilkins

CONTENTS

INTRODUCTION

Over the past forty years, I've written stories to emphasize a point with family members and friends, to give patients some "homework" to read and contemplate, for high school and college students in psychology and critical thinking, and for conference attendees' personal growth. I also write stories to clarify my own personal philosophies. I believe it makes a significant difference to do so. I encouraged all my students to read, write and think on a daily basis to enhance their own personal growth.

The first book I published was entitled <u>The Pocket Therapist</u>. It was published with the encouragement of R.L. Haley, Jr. in Connersville, Indiana at his Haley Press. Since that time, "Dock," as he was called, has died and his printing business is no longer in existence. It was a collection of stories, most of which had been published individually in professional journals and magazines in both the United States and Canada. It was pocket-size so as to be able to fit into a woman's purse or a man's suit pocket. Several thousand copies are in existence today. When Dock died, so did <u>The Pocket Therapist</u>.

In 2003, I decided to add some stories to <u>The Pocket Therapist</u> and it became <u>The Pocket Therapist, II</u>. I wrote it to be utilized by college students in my Strategic Thinking, Critical Thinking and Psychology courses at Hodges University in Fort Myers, Florida. The book has generated frequent, in-depth discussions in each and every class. Along with discussions, students have written thousands of critiques of the individual stories. Along with their critiques they have chosen to make personal comments stimulated by the "Food for Thought" at the end of each story. Often their comments and questions were such that I could not ignore them. I began to write individual responses to each and every student whose comments stirred something in me. That became almost another full time job.

I decided to add many of their personal comments, along with my analysis of their comments, to The Pocket Therapist, II and titled the book, Anatomy of Attitudes. It simply seemed like the appropriate thing to do. The idea is, a student reads a story (i.e., Puppets) and then responds, in a page or less, to the three bullets in "Food for Thought" at the end of the story. Then they submit those responses to me for my comments. My comments follow the students' comments in "Anatomy of Students' Attitudes."

College students say they like the idea because they "can not only read a story and 'get the message,' but they can read fellow students' thoughts and feelings and then get additional understanding from Doc's suggestions." The students in the classes I've taught ranged from 17 through 65 years of age. Therefore, the range of comments is wide and varied.

I decided that additions to The Pocket Therapist, II were absolutely necessary. I had received literally thousands of written comments from college students. The analysis of their attitudes seemed to be something that I could not ignore. It had to be done. Therefore, The Pocket Therapist, II became the Anatomy of Attitudes. And now, Help Yourself to Happiness: One Attitude at a Time.

PUPPETS

Article Saves Life: This story has an interesting history. After a radio interview, "Dr. Dave" left this story on the coffee table in the lobby as he was leaving the station. The station manager had planned to commit suicide that very evening. For reasons he could not explain, he noticed the paper as he left the building that evening and put it in his pocket. As he began to take his overdose of medication and drink the bourbon he bought on his way home that night, he started to read his copy of Puppets. He stopped attempting to die and called me on Monday morning to report that he was "alive and wanted to talk." He said the paper gave him the idea that "he had choices he never before believed."

Habits are those forces within us that direct us to behave the same way in the same situation. We learn to drink coffee in the morning before we do anything else. We learn that coffee is just not complete without a cylinder of paper stuffed with tobacco. We learn our habits so very well that soon we awake in the morning and are so well programmed that we find we are at work before we even realize that we are awake. We take a shower, brush our teeth, comb our hair, put on all those pastes and liquids, and never really stop to think about what we <u>really</u> want to do each step of the way. We simply practice till we have the procedure down so pat that we do not have to think about it any longer.

We learn to smoke and soon realize that every time we answer the phone we also automatically reach into our shirt pocket and search for a cigarette, without really wanting or deciding to have a cigarette. Answering the phone means to also have a cigarette. In fact, we find that on days when we have to answer the phone a great deal, we also smoke a great deal. That strange "force within us" has again taken over and we are once again puppets.

I am reminded of an old friend who used to bite his fingernails. He bit them with such vigor that his nails would no longer be bitable, so he would bite his skin. In fact, he bit his skin with such vigor that his fingers would bleed. I questioned him as to why he would continue to do that. I asked if it felt good. He said, "Of course not! It hurts, but it is a habit and I cannot stop!" It was clear to my friend, that this "strange inner force" had taken over his mouth and his teeth and he was unable to stop placing his fingers in his mouth … he was forced to bite and bite. Imagine this situation. My friend was unable to control his mouth, teeth and the muscles of his arms. His fingers were automatically placed in his mouth and he <u>had</u> to bite himself. Now that you have read these words for the second time I hope you understand his ridiculous attitude.

My friend was, in fact, <u>in control</u> of his hands. He did not have to bite himself. He <u>learned</u> to do this to himself at certain times, like when he was faced with a problem for which he did not have a quick solution. He practiced chewing on his fingers whenever he was nervous and the habit took over. When he was nervous, or thought he had a problem, he bit his nails. Soon he was "biting without thinking."

My friend believes that he has <u>always</u> bitten his nails, that he "is a nervous person", and he will always be a person who bites his nails. He is out of control! The habit has taken over! He got to the point of embarrassing himself with his nail-biting, so he hides his face and hands behind a book in order to let his habit continue without other people seeing what he is doing.

That is just the beginning of the list of habits that are out of control for human beings. How about these? "I cannot stop smoking, drinking alcohol, worrying about my children, arguing with my wife, eating candy, fighting with my roommate, driving too fast, thinking that others dislike me, crying when I see an animal hurt, getting angry when someone calls me a name, talking in class, getting into trouble with my teacher, believing that San Francisco will fall into the sea, thinking that I would be a better person if I had more self-confidence, wishing that I were rich, or wishing my spouse would behave as I want." We all have our own personal list of habits that "control us" and that we "cannot break."

The result of these attitudes is that we are "creatures of habit" and therefore "controlled by our habits." We are ***PUPPETS*** and should stop fighting these inner forces because they are always going to be within us and we might as well learn to live with them.

We could <u>choose</u> to not be satisfied being ***PUPPETS*** and learn to change our behavior. We can learn to behave, as we really would like to behave. We can make our habits work <u>for</u> us rather than against us.

I asked my friend whether he wanted to continue to be a finger-biting-puppet or whether he wanted to admit that he really did control what he put into his mouth … did he want to learn to stop biting himself? At this point, he chose not to get angry with me for referring to him as a puppet, and asked a question of me. He said, "You just used the word 'learned.' You said that I <u>learned</u> to bite my nails? So are you implying that I can <u>learn</u> not to bite myself?" I said that he was either <u>born</u> biting his nails <u>or</u> he learned this habit <u>after</u> birth. He could understand that when he was in the nursery as an infant, he probably did not bite his nails. Indeed, he remembered how he had started to bite his nails in college when the work got too intense. He could remember a time when he did not have the habit.

His new insight was that he <u>learned</u> to do something (bite his nails), and, therefore, he could <u>learn</u> not to do the very same thing. And so it is that we can change habits because (1) we once did not have the habit, and (2) we remember learning the behavior. We can rid ourselves of habits that we do not like. We can learn to have habits that are more in our best interest.

This means that there is <u>no</u> strange, uncontrollable force active within us to make us do things that we do not want to do. We

3

learn to act the way we do and we can, at any time, learn to behave differently.

My friend soon understood that he did <u>not</u> have to put his fingers in his mouth, and he did <u>not</u> have to bite himself. He could learn to keep his fingers out of his mouth and use his energy to do something he would enjoy. So it is with physical habits. We can train ourselves, through practice, to bite our nails, or not.

Are you thinking that this news is not really new to you? Are you thinking that it is very clear to you that <u>you</u> control where you put your hands, where you sit, when you stand, where you walk, and so on? If you were, I would say that most people probably agree with you. We learn physical habits and we can unlearn physical habits.

There are, however, two other categories of human behavior. The second is "cognitive" or "thinking" behavior. What about the thinking habits that we have … can we change our attitudes and beliefs? What about when you hear that people with a certain skin color are dangerous? We hear this from enough people and we may soon form the thinking habit, called an attitude or belief, that people with that particular skin color really are dangerous. Therefore the next time we see a person with that skin color we get frightened. We say, "That person frightened us!" but it was really our attitude that caused the fright.

We may think that mushrooms are bad to eat and we stay away from them and don't eat any. We think that people who like to read are not as worthy as people who play football and we see little value in the "bookworm." We think that college is too hard so we quit and never really give ourselves an opportunity to be successful. We think that teachers are people who are out to get us and we start to fight with them from the very beginning. We think that people with lots of money are better people than people with little money. We think, and we think, and we form attitudes that help us and some that work against us. I can remember thinking that I could not climb a mountain and so I never tried. One day I challenged that self-defeating belief and asked, "I think I can't and so I don't! But, I wonder if I could climb a mountain if I thought I could?" I began to practice the thought that I most likely <u>could</u>

climb a mountain if I had a mountain, the proper equipment, and the information as to how to climb. I went to North Carolina and asked the Outward Bound School to let me use their Table Rock. Indeed, I climbed the mountain and did it well!

I had lots of challenging thoughts after that. I started to challenge lots of attitudes I had about myself. I found many of them were highly inaccurate. I could do far more than I believed possible at the time. At least I could make the effort to find out.

Thus far we have discussed two of the three categories of human behavior. I know that I have both physical and cognitive habits, learned patterns of behavior that can be helpful or harmful. I know that I have learned to think and behave in ways that are in my best interest and that are self-defeating. And, I know that I have <u>choices</u> about how I think and physically behave. I can change my thoughts and my physical behavior. I am in charge of my thinking and my physical behavior!

The third classification of human behavior is emotive or emotional behavior. My brain also exercises ultimate control over my emotional behavior. This is where my friend started to disagree with me once again. He said that he found it impossible to believe that if someone called him a jackass he would not get angry. "In fact," he said, "I would go so far as to say that if someone calls me a jackass I <u>have</u> <u>to</u> get angry!" Let's look at this idea. He said that he has to get angry if someone says something to him that he does not like. Let's go back to the nursery for a moment. Let's imagine that we walk into a hospital nursery where newborn babies are waiting to be taken home. We walk into the nursery and say, "All you kids in here are a bunch of jackasses!" If the word "jackass" can make a human being angry then all the babies would be angry with us for calling them such a name. Of course this will not be the case. Do you know why? The babies will not be angry because they haven't <u>learned</u> to upset <u>themselves</u> having heard such a name. That's correct! I said <u>they have not yet learned</u> to upset themselves about the words that other people say to them. It's not the words that have magical power over another human being, but it's what we have <u>learned to think about</u> what other people say that causes our upset.

When I am sad, it is because I have learned a habit of upsetting myself when certain things happen around me. I learned to upset myself when someone I think is pretty tells me that she does not want to date me. I learned to upset myself when I don't get what I want. If I ask for a date and get the date, then I say "she made me happy." But I am the one that was in charge of my happiness because I could have chosen to be happy no matter what response I received. I could have said that I would like or prefer to have a date with this woman, but it would not be awful or terrible if she says no. If I tell myself that she <u>must</u> say "yes" if I ask her or I will be rejected and less of a man, then I will cause myself needless pain and suffering. I cause my pain and suffering depending on my own expectations and what I tell myself must happen.

Suppose that someone you define as "ugly" tells you she loves you. You will most likely not be happy with that pronouncement. If <u>words of love</u> make people happy, then you would be happy and not have a choice. You indeed have a choice in this case. You can be thrilled or frightened silly depending upon what you are saying to yourself about this person who says she loves you.

I remember the time a girlfriend told me that I made her happy when I gave her a box of candy. She actually made <u>herself</u> happy when I gave her the candy because <u>she</u> liked candy <u>and</u> she had a habit of thinking nice thoughts when someone gave her candy. Once she was on a secret diet to lose a few pounds to impress me with the way she looked. I went to see her with another box of candy, because the first box made such a positive impression. This time she got angry with me for being "so uncaring when she was working so very hard to diet!" She blamed me for upsetting her? It was really <u>her thoughts</u>, and not the sugar in a cardboard box, that were upsetting her. She did not know that <u>she</u> is responsible for the way <u>she</u> feels emotionally. She thought that <u>I</u> was in charge of her emotional life. The problem with that kind of thinking is that she will suffer needlessly. It is possible to be on a diet, receive a box of candy and not be upset. One could choose to save the candy for a later date. One could choose to be honest and explain that they are on a diet and the candy is only a negative temptation at the present time. One could accept the candy, throw it away and act appreciative. There are many choices other than upsetting oneself about a box of candy. And so it is with our emotional lives, we have many, many choices about what to think, and therefore how to feel.

We learn our habits … physical, cognitive and emotional. We can change the responses that we presently make. Just as we do not have to bite our nails, we do not have to be sad, angry, miserable and depressed when we do not want to be. People with healthy brains have control over all three areas of their behavior. Even when we think we are "out of control," we are really in control of how we are physically behaving, thinking and feeling.

The exciting fact is that we are <u>not</u> puppets controlled by our emotional habits, even when we think we are. We have control and we have choices! We can learn to exercise more efficient and effective control whenever we choose.

Allow me to explore one more idea with you. Imagine thinking that you are a "stupid person." You think and think and rethink the words, "I am a stupid person." If you practice this thought, you will eventually believe it. You will behave more and more like a stupid person should behave. You will behave in ways that support your thinking. You will come to <u>believe</u> that you <u>are</u> a stupid person even though you are not. You will be the same person you always were, but with a different attitude (thinking habit). You will now be the ***PUPPET*** of your "stupid habit." Your new attitude that you are stupid will keep you from trying things you'd like to attempt. Do you see what you have done? You have given yourself a new habit based on lies and you are using the lies to keep yourself from being successful.

Remember the mountain I wanted to climb? I told myself that I would love to try it but I am just not a mountain-climbing person! I told myself that I was not a mountain-climbing person and that belief kept me away from mountains. It became an attitude and therefore I never attempted to accomplish my desire. One day I examined my attitude regarding the kind of person who could climb a mountain. I thought about mountain climbing people. They had two legs, two arms, the proper equipment, a mountain and some mountain-climbing instructions. I had two legs, two arms, I could buy the needed equipment and I could borrow a mountain. I could indeed be "that kind of mountain-climbing person" whenever I wanted to be! Now I am!!

Have you read the book entitled <u>The Little Engine That Could</u>? The little train engine found that it could do much more than it ever thought possible if it practiced the thought, "I think I can, I think I can, I think I can!" I am not suggesting that you and I can do "anything" we think we can or "everything" we think we can. However, there is something that I have learned for myself, and that is that <u>I am capable of doing far more than I ever thought possible</u>. My potential is greater than I think. I bet there are still things I believe to be impossible that I could do, and do well. After successfully climbing Table Rock I know that my potential is far greater than I ever thought possible. That is exciting for me. It can be exciting for you also.

I believe that I can change the way I feel. I do not have to feel badly when others expect or demand I do. You can also believe that you can change the way you feel and you do not have to feel badly when others expect or demand you do.

You can do more than you believe possible at the present time. Give yourself a chance. Give yourself a new attitude. Try this one. Say "I <u>can</u> do <u>more</u> than I believe possible at the moment. I am <u>willing</u> to give myself the opportunity. I have <u>lots</u> of <u>choices</u>. I am a <u>powerful</u> person. I <u>can</u> change the way I <u>think</u>. I can <u>change</u> the way I behave. I can <u>change</u> my attitudes about the world and me, anytime I choose. I am a <u>valuable</u> human being and I <u>deserve</u> to treat myself better. I will start <u>now!</u>

Food For Thought

- Describe a habit that you would choose to modify, or eliminate completely, that has you behaving like a puppet.
- Why have you believed you have little or no control over the behavior?
- After reading this story, what have you learned that might give you the ability to change your seemingly unchangeable habit? Please be specific.

ANALYSIS OF ATTITUDES

"When my boyfriend comes home at a decent hour at night I will be happy. I have no control over when he comes home. I am angry when he stays out all night. I will try to break this habit but I pray he'll start coming home at a decent hour."

Get that <u>boy</u> out of your life. He's no friend! Then work on your <u>self-esteem</u>! He would rather be out all night with other people. He's <u>not</u> your friend. What you want is a real <u>friend</u>! Friends treat you with respect, not disrespect. Friends want to spend time with you, not run around and stay out all night.

And, praying to God is not going to change your "boyfriend's" behavior. The boy you describe is going to continue to take advantage of you as long as you allow it. My guess is that he comes home to you when his options are limited. He comes home to sleep with you when he can't sleep with someone else. I don't have positive regard for him, and neither should you.

You have to think highly of yourself. A true friend will think highly of you. <u>Your</u> attitude is important and you must believe that you <u>deserve</u> sincere, decent respect.

I care about you. I wish you cared more about yourself!

Doc

– – –

"A habit I would like to modify is the tremendous amount of junk food I consume. I would like to start eating a little healthier. I am going to try to learn to eat healthier."

This appears to be a non-goal. It means when you eat one less Twinkie a week, you will have "modified the tremendous amount of junk food" you consume and your goal will be reached. You don't <u>plan</u> to eat healthier. You plan to "try to learn" to eat healthier. Your goal is not clear and it is not specific. It is not doable.

How about this for your goal? I plan to stop eating ALL junk food for one day. I will design 3 nutritious meals and eat them as planned. I will do this for one day to prove to myself that it is possible. I know what good food is. I can eliminate all junk food from my life for one day. I will prepare some containers of sliced fruit and vegetables for snacks. I will plan on accomplishing this goal this Friday.

When I have succeeded with this goal, I will consider having another successful day on Saturday. I will have a successful day behind me and I can look in the mirror with self-pride. I will be on my way to becoming a healthier human being!

Congratulations …

Doc

— — —

"Maybe I should have more faith in myself."

Nah! I would recommend against it! I like the <u>low</u> self-esteem idea. Having <u>more</u> faith in <u>you</u> can lead to all kinds of problems. You may start to be more successful and your enjoyment of life may increase. You may notice that other people tend to take more of a liking to you and want to be your friends. You may also notice that your boss appreciates your work more and offers you a promotion. Of course you know that can lead to problems of what to do with the additional money on paydays. You may find that you are accomplishing things in your life that you never thought possible. And, the problems go on and on.

I do think it is better to stay as you are. (-:/

Doc

– – –

"The work for me doesn't end at five. When I get home from work I do homework with the kids, cook, do wash, give the kids a bath and get the kids' lunches and clothes ready for the next day. I feel there is not a moment to spare. When my husband comes home, he'll come over for a kiss and a hug. I'll be so into what needs to be done that I'll tend to push him away and say, "I'm busy!"

Life can be complex. Most of it we bring on ourselves. Perhaps you had enough on your plate before you decided to attend college? Perhaps your husband would be willing to take on some of the responsibility at night and give you a break? Perhaps you are taking too large a course load in college? There are certainly modifications that can and need to be made in your life. Conversations with your spouse might well be in order. I would suggest you talk with him and ask for his help and advice. I am confident that the two of you can construct workable plans together.

I think the idea of "together" is very important. Together we can do wonders! Together is a concept that most human beings prefer. Together is what you chose after you got acquainted with your husband, and I would assume that together is how you want to remain. Therefore, a "kiss and a hug" is something to look forward to, not a time push him away.

I am guessing that you are dealing with some resentment at the moment. I bet you resent the many chores for which you are responsible. You have more work than you can accomplish each day. You have a family, a full-time job, and are attending college at night. That sounds like 3 full-time jobs to me! If you are going to be successful, you need some help. Your partner needs to understand and support your goals. It is very important that you keep open communications with him. Ask for his support and help!

You also need to talk with your college advisor to determine whether or not you are taking a doable college load. Sometimes students put more on their plates than they can comfortably handle. An open and frank discussion ought to take place with your husband and college advisor.

Having a family, a full-time job and attending college is possible. It is usually not easy, but it is doable. With the help of your family and professional college advisement, your goals and dreams can become a reality.

I hope this advice will prove to be helpful.

Doc

— — —

"I bite my nails. But, I don't bite them after I spend $25 to get them done. If I don't bite them after spending $25 on them, I think I can not bite them at all."

I think you found a solution to your problem. If you have your fingernails done <u>twice</u> as often, then you will have good reason to never bite them. Ha! Seriously, you <u>do</u> understand that with good reason, you refuse to bite your nails. You are back in charge once again. You realize that you refrain from biting your fingernails after spending $25 on them, so you can <u>choose</u> to let them grow and look beautiful all the time. That's a very important insight.

You control what you put in your mouth and you have <u>stopped</u> doing so with your fingernails. Congratulations!!

Doc

— — —

"I am a horrible nail biter. I've bitten them since I was six. I can't even touch them because they hurt so badly. Perhaps I need to convince myself that I'm a valuable person and I should start treating myself that way."

"Perhaps" I need to convince myself that "I'm a valuable person." Perhaps you need to spend $25 a week getting them polished and that will put an end to your habit?

You're not "horrible," and you're not a "horrible nail biter." You may indeed have the habit of biting your fingernails. But, like so many other people, you can quit when you decide. Apparently, you didn't bite them before you were six, so you know of a time when you didn't have the habit. That helps.

Most people learned to bite their fingernails when nervous. You were apparently six years old when you started. You are an adult now. You understand you have an unwanted habit and you are in charge of the habit. You can stop biting your fingernails.

Perhaps you'd like to talk to someone about your nervousness, if indeed you think you are. Sometimes sharing one's thoughts with a professional counselor can make a positive difference. You have nothing to lose other than an unwanted habit. You might even come to the conclusion that you are indeed a valuable human being.

Doc

– – –

"I want to start something I want, and complete it through to the end. Sometimes I feel I have no control. People around me are always telling me that I can't do something, like go to college. I am a person with dreams. I can put my mind to do anything I want. I am a valuable person now, and will be at the end of the road."

The "feeling" of being out of control is really an **attitude** on your part. If you think you have no control in a situation then you "feel" powerless. You make the decision as to whether you start something and complete it. For the most part, that is your decision. When you "put your mind to it," you can do great and wonderful things.

You are a valuable person with exciting dreams and you deserve to experience some of your dreams coming true. Please choose not to listen to those around you who attempt to put a damper on your dreams. Those people are not your friends. Your friends will support your efforts to grow, learn and enjoy the world around you. Stick with your friends and put those with negative thoughts aside.

The world is an exciting place. It is waiting to be enjoyed. Go for it. (-:/

Doc

— — —

"One day I decided to examine my attitude about smoking. I came to the conclusion that I was the only one in charge of my habit! I was the only one that could put this habit out of my brain and out of my life. I am not a smoker anymore!"

Congratulations! I am <u>very</u> proud of your insight and the positive action you have taken to become a much healthier human being.

And, you have just made it a little harder for a tobacco executive to make his monthly BMW payment.

Keep up the **healthy** new habit!

Doc

— — —

"I know if I set my mind to it, I could actually quit smoking. I could stop, but I like it too much. Maybe the problem lies with me. Maybe I don't care enough about myself to undertake this task."

On the other hand, here is a person who is **not** determined to stop smoking! He could stop smoking **if** he put his mind to it, but his mind is elsewhere. He is not in a critical thinking mode, nor does it appear that he will be anytime soon! He could **stop** but he likes to **stink** from smoke and is comfortable with the thought of **dying** sooner. He thinks that **maybe** he could value himself more, but his present path of **self-destruction** is more appealing. He's a **drug addict**, but not concerned, because he's using a legal drug.

I wonder if he realizes that smoking cigarettes correlates highly with **low self-esteem**. I'll bet he started smoking to appear **mature**. What in the world is wrong with this picture?

Time to get real ... and back in control of your **attitude**!

Doc

— — —

"I felt rotten! I was the only girl in my church youth group to get pregnant before I was married. My friends and church members told me I was no good. I made a mistake and I was bad. They said that God was going to punish me and I would go to hell."

You are not rotten, nor can you become rotten! And, Chad cannot be rotten either. (Please read his story). Also, **stop** feeling rotten!!

God does not send people to hell for making mistakes; otherwise we'd all be there this very moment. We are **fallible** creatures. Fallible means that we are mistake-making creatures. No matter how hard we try, we cannot avoid making mistakes. Mistakes don't prove we are "bad," they prove we are **human**. Yes indeed, we are fallible human beings; mistake-making creatures.

It is important to **think for yourself!** It is important to understand **critical thinking** and do some everyday.

People come together in groups. The groups of people make rules for their organizations. The organizations expect us to follow their rules. Some are very strict and based on very old traditions. Some of the rules make sense, and others don't. Some are designed to keep us in line and out of trouble.

Some of the rules want us to behave according to the morals and values of the group. You admitted that it would have been better for you to have a child **later** in life. You "made a mistake." You didn't take the precautions that would have kept you from making a baby at an earlier age. You used poor judgment. The church agreed. They don't want young people having babies earlier in life than they believe proper. They created rules and scary stories to help prevent you from making mistakes. You can't really blame them for wanting to help direct your life. They mean well.

But sometimes the groups we belong to go a little overboard. They make up scary stuff like, "God is going to punish you and send you to hell!" I'm not sure what god they are referring to, but my God is a **loving** God. He does not send us to hell, nor punish us. We seem to do a good job of punishing ourselves without God's help. There seems to be no need for Him to also be nasty to us.

I wish boys and girls would not make babies. I wish they'd wait till they were responsible adults. My wishes don't make it so, and neither does trying to scare you.

Your baby needs a good mother. Please spend some quality time with your child everyday. Learn all you can about how to raise a healthy child and put your education to use in your family. **Be the best mother you can be** and enjoy your daughter. That will make both you <u>and</u> God smile.

You are a valuable, fallible human being. Love yourself and your child.

I wish you only the very best!

Doc Brown

— — —

"I always desire sweets. I believe that I have no control over wanting and purchasing them. Because I eat more than I need, I believe that I have no control over how much I should eat. I have learned by reading this story that the desire to eat large amounts of candy, cookies and other sweets is not something I was born with. It is a learned habit. I have learned that I have control over my actions in stores and I can stop myself from purchasing these sweet foods and stop myself from eating them. The story made me stop and realize that I have the ability to make the changes that will be beneficial to me."

Well said! I love when a fellow human being thinks critically. I am proud to have been a part of your new insight. Thanks!

Doc

— — —

"I have the habit of doing whatever people tell me to do. I automatically say yes. I don't think for myself. If I could change that, I would probably be better off."

It is **not** a case of "if." You can change when you choose. If you would be "better off" thinking for yourself, **do it!** Stand up for what <u>you</u> think.

Develop some backbone. Look in your mirror and see a positive, creative, powerful person! When you were born and came out of your mother, someone cut the umbilical cord that tied you to her. That meant you were free to move around on your own. Of course you were too weak, uneducated and dependent at the time. That is no longer the case. You are a free entity. You are free to move around. You are the captain of your own ship. Steer your ship in the direction **you** choose.

Get rid of your self-defeating habit. You are responsible for your life and the direction it takes. Stand up straight. Look around. See a world that is full of opportunity and excitement. Act as you think a positive and creative individual would. Think for yourself!

Practice saying, "No thanks, I prefer not to do as you are suggesting. I'm going to do it my way." Fake it, till you make it.

Doc

— — —

"I want to not react in a negative way when someone at work starts a rumor about me!"

Then, care <u>less</u> about what others say about you. People enjoy talking about other people. Folks with low self-esteem get their kicks by finding fault in others. Consider the source. People who are unhappy with who they are feel pumped-up by putting others down. It is a sick game they play, but nevertheless they play it.

If they are talking about me, they aren't talking about someone else. I'm doing someone else a favor. Ha! Besides, I work to earn money to do the things I want to do on my days off. I have an agreement with my supervisor. I work 8 hours for 8 hours pay. I do my job better than she expects and she pays me when she promised. It works well that way. I don't have time to listen to see if other people are talking about me. I simply don't care.

Someone once said to me, "I heard you have been married 5 times! You are a psychologist and I think that's awful." I turned to them and said, "Five times? You heard wrong. I believe the number is six." She was not asking for information from me. She was telling me what she believed and what she thought, based on her beliefs. As long as she was being rude and asking me for personal information, I thought I would give her something "additional" to think about.

I have no worries about what you say behind my back. I live life according to my values and expectations. I don't have to live as you do. You are free to choose your path. We live differently. Evaluate my behavior if and when you choose. It is OK with me.

Take life less seriously. Do your job. Live your life. Enjoy something everyday. Your critics will always be there. So what!

Doc

– – –

"My problem is I think I am not good enough for well-paying jobs. I only apply for jobs in the fast-food industry."

Millions of people in the world think they're not good enough. I wonder how we got that way. Maybe we listened to negative parents, teachers and peers while growing up. Maybe we have a tendency to think poorly of ourselves without outside help. Some people told us we are sinners and tainted from the very beginning. We're told to seek forgiveness on a weekly basis.

OK, I see! So we had a negative start. But, it is a **new day today.** It is the first day of the rest of our lives! I can **change my mind.** I'm a good person. I have nothing to dislike myself for today! **I am honest, dependable, trustworthy, hardworking, and deserve an opportunity to put my skills to work**. I can **believe** these things about myself and **act** as though I do.

Life isn't easy, but it's **doable**. I can apply for higher paying jobs than the fast-food industry provides. I can get more education. I can ask for training. I can work diligently and prove my worth to an employer.

"Hey, I'm good enough! I have lots of potential and I am not afraid to work hard. I want to learn and increase my skills in the world-of-work. I will create opportunities for myself. I will start today!"

Doc

HELP YOURSELF TO HAPPINESS

— — —

"I commit to stop biting my nails today!"

<u>Congratulations</u>! A new habit begins with (1) deciding that there is something about yourself that you don't like and want to change, and (2) making the direct decision to **stop** doing what you did, and **start** behaving in the new way.

Thanks for sharing!

Doc

— — —

"I am too busy to lose weight. I don't have time to exercise. If I started exercising, I would just be interrupted. I don't like exercise anyway. If I try to think of it as something I want to do, it might make it easier to exercise."

It is clear that you are not going to be losing weight anytime soon! You're too busy. You don't have time. You don't want to exercise. You don't even want to think about losing weight. Forget about it.

Or, perhaps you could **care about yourself**. If you cared about yourself, you'd think about the benefits of eating a balanced diet and exercising. If you thought you were worth it, you'd care about everything you do to yourself.

Ah, never mind! You're too busy! You don't have time! You don't deserve it! Doc

— — —

"One habit I would like to eliminate is my feelings of racial tension that I've felt since moving to Fort Myers. I heard two of my coworkers make a racially biased comment about African American people. I quit my job. I was uncomfortable. I also began to feel very uncomfortable around all white people. I started to think that all white people have the same views."

19

We are all brothers and sisters under the skin. There will always be negative, rude, aggressive, mean, nasty, uneducated, defective, sick individuals in this world. We will encounter them from time to time.

Dr. Abe Maslow suggested I place a bright, orange, flashing, neon "B" on the forehead of each such individual I meet. The "Bs" can only be seen by me, and I can see them coming from miles away. I don't have to be surprised to see one coming because I put it there. I don't have to be surprised when he once again acts as he did in the past. He is a "B" and I expect him to act that way.

It helps reduce my tension. He is what he is and I accept him the way he is. I don't have to "like" his behavior, but I accept it coming from him. I sure don't have to change my lifestyle because he is in my world. I don't have to quit my job because there are individuals around that talk about me behind my back. The odds are that someone always will. I can live with it!

I wish all the people of my world were nice, but they aren't. That's a fact, Jack! Ha! So deal with it. Accept the idea that people have imperfections. It can make life **inconvenient** at times, not awful. Sometimes the "Bs" can make life **damned inconvenient**, but still not terrible. I can stand some inconveniences in my life! So can you.

It takes some practice not to exaggerate what happens to us. We have a tendency to embellish the negative. A couple of people talk behind my back. I find out about it. I think no one likes me. I think about it for a few days and decide that I cannot work for a company where no one likes me. I quit! The problem is I got the worst of the deal.

None... All... Never... Always ... can be self-defeating words. Watch out for them in your vocabulary. You're a good and worthwhile person. Do not punish yourself without damn good reason!

Doc

– – –

"It was hard! Many times I wanted to give up! I never did though. I lied to myself. I told myself that I liked wrestling and kept practicing. I started to win and the harder I practiced the more matches I won

and the more people I defeated. **By the time my senior year came, I was a 4-year varsity letterman. I placed in 9 tournaments and took a 3rd in the state championship. I will never forget!"**

You didn't really "lie" to yourself. You told yourself what you wanted to believe. There is a significant difference. You wanted to be a quality wrestler. You were having difficulty. You talked to yourself in a positive manner and it helped make you successful. It isn't rocket science; it is some simple psychology. Want to be successful? Talk to yourself as a successful person talks.

You started to win. The more you practiced, the more you won. Dr. George Axtelle said, "The harder I worked, the luckier I got." Hard work and practice pays off.

Remember how you did it then. Do it again today. College is **doable** for you. See you at graduation!

Doc

— — —

"I am the biggest procrastinator! Everyday that goes by is just another wasted day. I just keep telling myself I'll do it later or I will do it tomorrow. This way of thinking has caused my life to be more hectic than it needs to be."

Wonderful! You know what the problem is and you know how you got here. Now reverse the process. **You're in charge!** Buy an appointment book. A month-at-a-glance calendar will do just fine. Choose an assignment you want to accomplish. You have to read a chapter in your text and write chapter notes. Pick a couple of free times in your schedule tomorrow and make notes in your appointment book. "From 10:00 a.m. until 11:00 a.m. tomorrow morning I will read Chapter One in my psychology book. From 8:00 p.m. until 8:30 p.m. I will write my chapter notes." Now you have a specific plan and it is written in your appointment book. Tomorrow, do as you planned. When you have accomplished those two tasks, you will no longer be "the biggest procrastinator."

Follow that pattern five days a week. Assign times to read, write and think about your coursework daily. Stick to your schedule. Procrastination will become a thing of your past. Congratulations!

Doc

— — —

"I want to change my habit, but I think it will be difficult!"

Henry Ford is quoted as saying, "If you think you can't, you can't. If you think you can, you can!" Changing a habit is not difficult. It is **doable**. Change requires you to (1) <u>decide that you don't like something you are presently doing and you want to change</u> from it. Next you need to (2) <u>make a direct decision to change</u>.

Write down on paper, as clearly as possible, what you would like to do differently. Write down all the reasons why it would be good to change your behavior. Record how you think you would feel with the new habit. Pick a date and time to begin your new behavior. "Tomorrow morning when I get up, I will _____." You must not only **act** in the new manner, you must **think** in a manner that supports the new habit. I choose not to have the cigarette I usually would have this morning. That's the **action**. "I am proud to be a non-smoker! I am in control of what I put in my mouth and cigarettes will never again be one of them. This is a wonderful new smoke-free path I am on. I can already imagine my body repairing itself. I like being a non-smoker!" That's an example of the **new thinking** needed to support your new behavior. **The thinking will make it so.**

Doc

— — —

"Why are habits so hard to break? Everyday after work, I habitually drink a few beers and melt into my lazy chair. The only movement for at least two hours is my thumb against the remote control on the television."

Sounds like you have learned to "chill out" after work. Want to change it? Make a personal decision today to arrive home from work tomorrow, take a shower, and read a chapter from your assigned homework. Think about your change of behavior during the day. Smile with the thought **you are taking charge** and making some personal changes in your life.

Tomorrow when you arrive home after work, take a shower, get a cold drink for yourself (not beer), and read for an hour. Read, write and think about your coursework for an hour each day, five days a week. After completing your homework, you may indeed reward yourself with a beer.

Now your old habit is behind you, and you're on a path toward college graduation.

Doc

— — —

"I have road rage. I hate when people don't drive the speed limit! I get pissed off and tailgate them or beep at them until they move. I believe I have little control over my behavior."

Sounds to me like <u>you</u> have a <u>death wish</u>! The highways do <u>not</u> belong to you. They are a <u>shared</u> property with millions of Americans and visitors to our country. When other people don't drive as <u>you</u> expect, <u>you</u> upset <u>yourself</u> and put us all in danger. What gives <u>you</u>, or anyone for that matter, the right to endanger another person's life? You are acting like a brat and I suggest for everyone's sake, you grow up and drive responsibly and respectfully immediately!

You only have one life to live and you endanger yourself when you act this way. I respect you on the highway and I ask you to respect me. You are <u>not</u> without fault behind the wheel and neither am I. We all make mistakes when we drive. If I show you courtesy, and you do the same, we just might live to drive yet another day.

How about it!? Rage <u>not</u>.

Doc

FEELINGS

Feelings are talked about, sung about, written about, and are learned by each of us from birth to death. They are the joy we search for and the suffering we experience. Yet most human beings behave and talk as though feelings control <u>them</u>, rather than they control the feelings. We talk of feelings as being out of control; of being overcome with feelings; being disabled with feelings; punished by them; backed into a corner by them; and used by them. And yet, the truth is we learn to have the emotions that we harbor. Emotions are learned behaviors. We learn how to be angry, how to look when angry, how to sound when angry, who to be angry with, and how long to stay angry. We learn how to hurt, we learn how to look hurt, and we learn what to hurt ourselves about and how long to stay hurt. We learn to punish ourselves. We learn to punish ourselves when others behave in a manner that is contrary to what we expect. We believe that others should do what we want, rather than what they want. We punish ourselves because they have not done what we think they should have done.

Were I responsible for the creation of mankind, then perhaps, and only perhaps, would I be able to dictate to humans what they ought, should, must be doing at any particular time. However, if I am not the creator of mankind, then most likely each human being has the right to behave as he thinks he ought to behave. Therefore, I do <u>not</u> have the right to demand that my fellow man behave as <u>I</u> think he should. The next step in this thought process is, "I also do not have to punish myself because my fellow man behaves as he thinks is rational for him."

There seems to be a "conflict" that humans are taught to experience. Conflict, as I define it, is the <u>difference</u> between what really is happening

24

and what one would like to have happening. This is where our destructive emotions come into play. I see the world not as it really is, but colored by my attitudes and beliefs. As my beliefs become more subjective, based upon my opinions rather than reality, I suffer. As my beliefs become reality oriented and more in line with what is <u>really</u> happening, then I seem to suffer far less. The two circles move closer together. One circle contains "what I see as reality" and the other circle contains "how I expect or want things to be in my life." The less subjectively I learn to think, and the more reality-oriented I become, the more my feelings reflect a true picture of what is really happening to me.

Take for example the common belief that one <u>must</u> be loved and approved of by everyone in order to be happy. If I believe this idea, then I have to suffer self-punishment when a fellow human being exercises his right not to like me or disapproves of me. I learn to think of myself as a less-valuable human being when an acquaintance chooses not to associate with me any longer. I choose to think less of myself when a loved one chooses to no longer love me. However, the reality of life is that I am not worth more or less, dependent on the number of friends, lovers, acquaintances, etc., that I have. I am still the fallible human being that I was when I was born and that I will continue to be. Should my family choose to no longer value being with me, I am still a valuable, worthwhile human being who can experience peace and happiness. My happiness is <u>not</u> dependent on who loves me and who approves of my behavior.

My happiness in life is dependent on the <u>thoughts</u> that I use to evaluate my perceptions of reality. The reality <u>is</u> that <u>I</u> control my feelings by what I think about me and about my relationships with others. If I choose to think and believe that <u>others</u> control how I feel, then I have to work on changing other people's behavior. If I rather choose to think and believe the reality that <u>I</u> make my own happiness by thinking and believing reality-oriented thoughts, then I find a new world filled with relative peace and happiness.

If I choose to think that it would be <u>nice</u> if people loved me and approved of my behavior, but don't <u>have</u> to love and approve of me, then

I find I am freed of the "must" syndrome that is the cause of so much emotional pain. People may choose their own friends according to their own desires and wishes, and they do not have to choose me!

If I choose to think that people behave, as <u>they</u> want, and not as I want, then I can free myself from some negative feelings. Feelings can be an exciting part of the human experience, and they can also be the "hell" of life. The fact of the matter is that <u>we</u> control the amount of happiness or hell that we experience in life.

The human brain is the most important single organ in the human body. It is there we learn to respond to our environment and it is the brain that controls our behavior. However, my brain is only going to produce outcomes for me dependent on the information I choose to feed it. If I choose to believe lies and false information, then I experience feelings based on false data. My brain can believe that the world is flat if I choose to practice flat-world thoughts. My brain can believe that my mother and father <u>must</u> love and approve of me for me to be happy. But, just because I believe this idea does not make it true! If I believe it's true, then I will suffer when it does not happen. My brain may believe that should a loved one choose to live with someone else that my heart will break in two, but the belief does not make it true! I can believe that there is only one woman in the world that I can love, but my belief does not make it true!

I am the cause of my suffering, my negative emotions, and also my happiness and contentment. The more my thinking is in touch with REALITY, the less I will suffer. Because I LEARNED to have feelings that are self-destructive, I can RE-EDUCATE myself to have feelings that are more in my best interest.

The question as to whether I am dealing with what I THINK is real as opposed to what IS real is crucial to my mental health. The 18-year-old girl who once told me that "her mother could make her unhappy whenever she wanted to, and keep her that way as long as she wanted to" was expressing a very "real", but untrue belief. But as long as she chose to believe that idea, she had to feel badly when her mother disapproved of her behavior. When she learned that it was IMPOSSIBLE for her mother to make her angry, or to keep her that way, her life changed significantly. She learned that her belief was NOT in line with reality, but rather what she thought was reality. There is often a difference! She learned that she did not have to punish herself simply because her mother evaluated her behavior in a negative fashion. She did not need her mother's approval all of the time to be a happy, contented daughter. The daughter was responsible for her own emotional life and her BELIEF SYSTEM about herself and her mother controlled it.

The woman who told me that "she could not go on without a husband" was expressing her opinion and NOT reality. The man who said "he had nothing to live for now that the only woman he could ever love had left him" was also expressing his own opinion and NOT reality.

Thinking objectively may be relatively new for some people, but it is not impossible. It may be a new mental (thinking) habit that can be learned with practice. It is up to each individual to PRACTICE the new thinking until the old belief is extinguished. The world is as it is, and we can choose to deal with it as it is and experience less misery, or we can choose to imagine the world differently from the way it is and suffer more.

If we look around us, it seems to be in vogue to suffer and express a significant degree of misery when life does not treat us as we prefer. But, just because other people expect us to be miserable when they are, is no reason for us to comply with their expectations!

Critics of this thesis object on the grounds that human beings become "machines that give up their emotional lives." This is an empty criticism. Human beings are EMOTIONAL beings who will continue to have emotions (feelings) as long as they are alive. Rather, what I believe is that because emotions are LEARNED behaviors, we can LEARN to have feelings that are more in our own best interest. WE can LEARN to be HAPPIER and less miserable. We can LEARN to give up the nonsense that we believe and replace our negative feelings with more pleasant feelings.

Can you remember a time when you did not have a lover and you were a worthwhile human being? Can you remember a time when a particular person did not love you and you were still worthwhile? If you can remember such times, then you can believe that the same is true <u>now</u>. If you cannot remember a time in the past when such was true, then you can learn for the first time that we <u>are</u> valuable <u>and</u> worthwhile with or without lovers, approvers, and certain particular friends.

We need to eat, drink water, keep relatively warm in the winter and cool in the summer, and what else? We can evaluate what it is that we REALLY NEED, versus what we only WANT. We do NOT have to have EVERYTHING we want in order to have peace and contentment! However, if we choose to believe that we NEED all those things that we only want, then we have to suffer more than necessary.

If you tell yourself that you want to be happier and less miserable, then also tell yourself that you CAN, whenever you choose to begin. Begin NOW. You CAN start to argue with yourself as to what you need versus what you only want. You can start by filtering or sifting your thoughts through an objective, factual, reality-oriented screen to allow yourself to have feelings that are more in line with reality. You can start by telling yourself that people have the right to behave, as <u>they</u> want. They do not have to behave, as <u>you</u> want. You don't have to believe all subjective opinions you now believe. You can start telling yourself that <u>you</u> have <u>equal worth and value</u> as much as any other human being around you. You can start feeling less miserable <u>today</u> by thinking <u>your</u> feelings are <u>not</u> controlled by other people. <u>Your</u> attitudes and beliefs make <u>you</u> feel the way you do! You can give-up your self-defeating attitudes and beliefs for ones that feel better, whenever you choose!!

You can start by thinking that life is filled with lots of choices. You can start feeling the way you want to feel anytime you choose to think objectively. The choice is yours to make. You can feel the way you want to feel anytime you want. You only have to be controlled by others as long as you choose to believe it is possible. Indeed, your feelings are really yours. You have created them and only you can keep them the way they are, or give them up for more comfortable feelings.

The CHOICE and the DECISION are YOURS . . .

HELP YOURSELF TO HAPPINESS . . . START TODAY.

Food For Thought

- Perception is a <u>combination</u> of what we sense <u>plus</u> our personal evaluation of our senses. It appears that we don't deal with reality; we deal with <u>perceived</u> reality. Our feelings are dependent on our perceived reality. Therefore our feelings are often exaggerated. When we reevaluate what has happened to us, our perceptions change, as do our feelings. When have you <u>reevaluated</u> an event in your life to understand it more accurately, and therefore have less unhappy feelings? Please be specific.
- "I am the cause of my suffering." Have you had this insight recently? What did you think or do differently?
- Our lives are indeed full of <u>choices</u>. What choices have you exercised recently to make positive changes in your life?

ANALYSIS OF ATTITUDES

"I think it's very good that you think positive. I would like to understand why so few of us are able to think positively. The first thought for me would tend to be negative, and if I'm lucky, I look for a positive outcome in a given situation. I don't think one is able to make the choice instantaneously. It seems we are programmed to go one way or the other, positive or negative. Nature versus nurture must have something to do with it. Most people think negative. I wonder why you are able to think positive so easily, not like most of us. There must be a reason. For you it may come naturally, but it seems impossible for most of us. Why is that? You might be that rare individual that needs to be studied. Compare your MRIs with others. Maybe you have more serotonin or dopamine in your head.

Lucky you! Positive thinking just does not come naturally. It's just not easy. The human brain is just so different in everyone. You have a rare gift, the ability to automatically think positive!

First, I believe that anyone and everyone, with a healthy brain, has the ability to think positively and/or negatively. I believe it is a personal choice. The great minds that I know agree with me. Recent research indicates that Americans have learned to do more negative thinking than positive thinking, but it remains a personal choice. Your ability to think positive thoughts is equal to your ability to think negative thoughts. Your choice is where you would like to focus. It is just as "easy" to think something positive as it is to think something negative.

I believe that if your first thoughts tend to be negative, then we can assume that you learned that thinking habit. The important point is that you learned to have the habit. Re-education is possible for you. That should be good news for you, and everyone else.

You don't have to be "lucky" to have a positive outlook, but you do need determination and practice. You and I must **LOOK** for the **POSITIVE** side of the situation. If life hands us lemons, we must consider making lemonade. We can choose to "bitch, moan, and groan," or we can whistle a happy tune. Sound silly? It's our **CHOICE**. You know that the glass, when half-full, is also half-empty. Which do you want to see? One brings you down, the other lifts you up. What's my choice? I prefer being **UP!** I know, you are saying, "Well, it's just not that easy." Leave "easy" out of it! Where do you want to be? How do you want to feel most of the time? What do you deserve? Those are the questions to be answered.

I want to feel that my life is worth something, so I have to look for and find the positive aspects of my life. They are there to be found! I want to be happy, most of the time. I have to look for those aspects of my life that are uplifting and cause me to smile. They are there to be found, for you and me.

I want to be acceptable to me. I can look in a mirror and like what I see. Sure there are "improvements" that I would like to make, but I am acceptable at the moment. I like what I see in the mirror, and why not? You can look in your mirror and like what you see. Why not? Not liking oneself is just kind of silly. Say, "I like what I see!" Say it like you want to mean it! Say it like it is important to your mental health, your self-concept and your self-image. If I don't like me, how in the world can I expect someone else to like me? Practice till you get it right. I deserve to like me and feel good about me. You deserve to like yourself and feel good about yourself. Write this down! Say it to yourself!! Write it a thousand times, until you believe it!!! Tell your friends, "I like me!" That will make you, and them, smile. There is nothing wrong with a few smiles.

The only thing you get "quickly" is trouble. Re-education does not happen instantaneously. It takes practice, but it is **DOABLE**.

We are "programmed" to sweat when the air around us is hot. We aren't "programmed" to be happy or sad. We aren't "programmed" to be positive or negative. It is our personal choice. You form habits. You know about habits. You have lots of them. You seem to think you were <u>born</u> being a negative thinker. I am here to inform you that negative thinking is a **HABIT**. That's really hopeful because **YOU CAN CHANGE**. You can see the positive side of life, when you choose to. It is there to be seen.

I just thought of a great professor I had in San Diego many years ago. You would benefit by reading one of his books. He wrote <u>Man's Search for Meaning</u>, and his name is Dr. Viktor Frankl. He had more reasons than you and I put together to be negative, and he chose to be positive. I highly recommend his book to you. If he did what he said he did, you and I can also be positive thinkers!

There are lots of valuable books about the human brain. If you researched some, you would learn that we aren't born with happiness or sadness as predetermined paths in life. Happiness and sadness are personal choices. When I was in undergraduate school, I was a member of the AFROTC Drill Team. We were invited to a Spring Drill Team Competition in Mississippi at an Air Force Base. The day after we arrived we were invited to visit New Orleans. I was excited because when we arrived on Bourbon Street I thought I saw a float and a band coming towards us. I thought it to be part of the Mardi Gras. I told our host that I wanted to watch what was going on. I thought there was a parade about to begin. Our guide laughed at me! He said, "That's not a parade, it is a funeral procession." But they were so happy and the music was so upbeat! How could it be a funeral? Our guide explained, "In the South, death is treated as a celebration. It is believed that the deceased has left the 'hell of earth' and is going to a better, more peaceful place."

That was certainly not what I was used to while living in Cleveland, Ohio. Death was a time of sadness, regret and loss. So if we believe one way, we are sad? If we believe another way, we have feelings of joy and relief? It must not be the <u>event</u> that produces the feelings, but rather the <u>thoughts we think about the event</u> that cause our sadness or joy. So then, I can choose to think whatever is in my best interest about an event and feel the way I want to feel. I like that ability!

I do not have a "rare ability," or an ability that you don't have. You and I have the same abilities when it comes to choices about positive and negative thinking. The difference is in our habits, not in our abilities. Hurrah for us!!

If we are trying to understand why a person has the 'gift' of positive thought, we might acknowledge that he may have been lucky enough to develop under the tutelage of a wise teacher. Then parlaying that tutelage with his innate sense of wisdom he is in a position to live wisely.

The 'gift' may come from anyone, anywhere. You may find it in your mom, your fourth grade teacher, your choir director, or, who knows. The source of the gift may be someone who is living a model life or someone who knows how to explain his deepest thoughts.

When you sense that you are in the presence of a positive personality you will know that you have the opportunity to choose an attitude to bolster your <u>own</u> psyche.

Both my parents were positive, hardworking, loving people. I've been able to find positive reasons to emulate my elders and some of my teachers. I was fortunate enough to have a mathematics teacher and an English teacher at Euclid High School who were very positive in both their ideas and behavior. They were inspirations to me. Life away at college was very positive. It gave me the opportunity to follow men and women such as Bernice Roberts, Bill Wilkins, Abe Maslow, Viktor Frankl and George Axtelle. These incredible examples of positive thinking gave me the privilege of standing on their shoulders to see the world from their perspectives. I have been ever grateful for the opportunities.

I work at seeing the positive side of situations everyday. I am enthusiastic about it. It does not come naturally. It is not my habit because of some excess in brain chemicals. The gift may indeed be the ability to think, to reason, and to do both in positive ways. But, it is my **CHOICE** to **LOOK** for the **POSITIVE ASPECTS of MY LIFE.**

You have the same ability, and you are free to start today to have a more positive outlook. Make a list. List anything and everything positive in your life. Be enthusiastic and eager to find positive things to put on your list. Even the "little things" count. List them, all of them. You may ask your friends and family to help you with your list. "What do you see as positive aspects of my life? What things have you seen me do that have been positive? How have you seen me be kind, loving and gentle to others? What have you seen me do that you consider positive? How have I treated you in a positive way?"

Make a list. Add to it each and everyday. Read your list before bed each night. Feel good about what you have done. Smile at yourself in your mirror and say, "Well done!"

Positive thinking is not controlled by the government. There are no taxes on positive thoughts. There is no law against it. It is **FREE** for the **TAKING.**

HELP YOURSELF to HAPPINESS.

I wish you only the very best!

Doc Brown

– – –

"I love my boyfriend more than I could ever express in words. But ... over the past two years I have learned to not pay attention to him. I listen to him, but I no longer take what he says to heart because he shoots down my hopes and dreams."

I believe it is TIME to express in words WHY you have loving feelings for a man who shoots down your hopes and dreams! It is TIME to express in words WHY you have loving feelings for someone you have learned to ignore. Is he the very last man on earth? You have no choice about being with him? I don't think so.

Love has reasons. I believe love ought to be explainable, real, alive, growthful, definable, and defensible, make rational sense, and be supported with critical thinking. Why not?

Love is a feeling, an emotion. It appears in the human brain when loving thoughts create it. There are thoughts, attitudes, and beliefs that define the feeling called "Love." It isn't there because of some mysterious force. "He" didn't put it in your brain and there is nothing you can do to change it. Your feeling of "love" is inside you because you gave it reason to be there. No magic. Real human cognition creates a loving feeling. It's the thinking that makes it so.

Perhaps you thought you loved him when he was behaving as you wanted. Now he is showing his true colors and you are afraid to think that he is not the man for you? Relationships are not easy. They are complex. It takes time and experiences to learn what your partner is really like. Infatuation does not do that. Time, research, and experience tell us what we really need to know.

Often we don't want to know. We ignore or try not to notice what reality is telling us. Our friends think we are happy. They see us together. They think of us as a couple. We say we are happy when we aren't. We say that we love him or her more than words can explain, when we really know the words to explain how we feel, we just don't want to face reality. It's hard to break the habit of being together … of being a couple. The momentum is seemingly hard to overcome, but needs to be overcome.

You might be thinking, "It won't be easy to find another partner. It will take work. I'll have to start all over again. How will I support myself by myself? It was no fun to be alone before he came along. He is better than nothing. What will my friends think? How will I face my parents and friends? They really don't know him and they will think I've lost my mind! Maybe he's right. Maybe I shouldn't have hopes and dreams. Maybe he is enough for me. If I would just listen to him, everything would be all right."

Maybe it is TIME to THINK for YOU and ABOUT you. It is TIME for you to DEFINE the idea of your love for your boyfriend.

The odds are he is not going to change for you. The odds are your hopes and dreams are not going to change because he does not support them. I believe you have the right to define your hopes and dreams, and work to make them become reality. A partner with some of the same hopes and dreams would be very exciting. You would not have to "ignore him." Wow!

There are good partners out there. They may not be waiting on your front porch, but they are out there. Some of them are even looking for you. Can you believe that? I suggest you think about it.

I actually feel a little sick inside when I read comments like yours. I believe you have a right to be content. I believe you have the right to pursue your dreams. I believe you have the right to look for a partner if you choose to have one. You claim you have a boy "friend" who seems to not be a "friend" at all. Love ought to start with a great friendship. I think you ought to look for a friend. Define what you want in a friend. Write down all the requirements. Insist on someone who supports your hopes and dreams. Insist on someone who supports what you like and enjoy. Look for a compatible partner. Insist that your "love" is going to depend on getting most of the requirements you desire in a partner.

YOU are a SPECIAL human being and YOU DESERVE SOMEONE SPECIAL. I bet I could travel to most any street corner in this country and find someone who would not support my hopes and dreams in life. That ought to be easy. You can find lots of them, easily. Look for SOMEONE SPECIAL.

YOU are SPECIAL! (I know I just said that, but it's important that you think about it.) Think about it … often.

Doc

– – –

"What upsets me is, out of all the people that I work with, only a few pull their weight!"

Allow me to get right to the point. The "people who don't pull their weight" are not the cause of your upset. Your belief that, "Other people in the company must work like I do!" is. When they don't meet your expectations, you upset yourself. You must believe other people are put on this planet to do as you demand. That is not the case, and you know it.

Dr. Albert Ellis, a famous psychologist, once said, "Other people do what they want, not what I want, and I do not have to upset myself when they do." You work 8 hours a day for 8 hours pay. You do the best you know how to do and make every effort to meet your boss' expectations. You have plenty to do at your place of business without upsetting yourself because other employees are not as conscientious as you. Let your boss manage the other employees. You do your job and stop upsetting yourself about what others are doing, or not doing.

"But it is not fair!" I imagine this is what you are thinking now that I've suggested you do your job and let other people fend for themselves. Actually, there are only two kinds of fair. One is the "County Fair," and the other is the "State Fair." The issue you are concerned about has nothing to do with fairness. There was never an agreement signed saying, "We will all pull our own weight!" You just made it up in your mind and expect other employees to follow your expectations.

Go to work. Do what you agreed to do for the company. Be an example to other employees who need a model to follow. Earn your paycheck. Use your energy to find something positive in your day and thereby produce some personal enjoyment for yourself. Allow other people to do as they choose.

Help yourself to some peace and calm, and upset yourself less about the behavior of others. Makes sense to me. Try it, you might like it.

Doc

– – –

"A good friend of mine upset me when she thought I had lied to her."

"A good friend of mine upset me." I know you believe this statement to be fact, but it is not possible for your friend to upset you. You are the one that upsets you, and the only one who can. When you learned your friend was upset with you, <u>you</u> decided to also feel upset.

We ought to take responsibility for our feelings. My feelings are just that, <u>my</u> feelings. <u>Your</u> feelings belong to you. You decide when to upset yourself. You decide what to get upset about. You learned how to look and act when upset. You decide how long to stay that way. You have far more responsibility than you presently believe.

I understand you told your friend something. She chose not to believe you, for whatever reason. She thought you lied to her. It may well have happened just like that. It was <u>not</u> awful or terrible. It may have been <u>inconvenient</u>, or even darn inconvenient, for your friend not to believe you. We'd all like other people to believe what we tell them. Sometimes, or often, they don't. So then what? Come home and kick the dog? Get drunk? Slap ourselves in the face? Burn down the house? Or, upset ourselves because other people do what they have the right to do? We have choices, you know. You could choose to say, "I told you the truth. I didn't lie to you. The ball is in your court. When you choose to believe what I said, call me. Until then, I am a busy woman with lots to do." You could <u>choose</u> to say these things in a factual manner with little or no upset on your part. Think about it.

You and I have lots of choices about how we respond to others. You ask me a question. I give you an answer. You don't like the answer I gave you, that's your choice. You don't have to like everything I do. I don't have to upset myself because you don't like my behavior. You and I have choices about how we respond to everything that happens to us.

<u>Other people do what *they* want, not what I want. I don't have to upset myself when they do.</u> Besides, I am too nice a person to upset myself without damn good reason! I really do believe many people have learned to look for reasons to feel upset. Somehow they think it is normal for them. "Life is upsetting," and they suffer accordingly.

I believe it makes sense to feel as good as possible, as often as possible. So let's you and I <u>look for reasons to feel good</u>, while ignoring reasons to feel badly. We'd feel better, would we not? Isn't that the point? We cannot please all the people all the time, not even family and close friends. Other people have the choice to upset themselves, and they can use us as their reasons.

I choose not to make me feel worse than absolutely necessary. How bout you?

Thanks for asking,

Doc Brown

— — —

"My girlfriend really upset me recently! She chose her boyfriend over me. Ever since we were little, we always said that our boyfriends would never come between us."

You are not "little" anymore! Promises made when you were little tend to change when you reach adulthood. Do <u>you</u> plan to love your girlfriend more than your boyfriend or husband?

It wasn't your girlfriend who upset you. <u>You</u> upset <u>you</u>, because a promise made by two children was not honored in adulthood. You may find this odd, but I remember telling a girl in the second grade I loved her and wanted to be with her forever. Today, I don't remember her name, but I do remember that she made a wonderful, second-grade-impression on me. I expected to keep my promise at the time, but life changed and so did my promise.

I most likely promised my mom and dad I would never, ever leave them. I made them promise they would never leave me. One day I met another wonderful woman, one with whom I wanted to spend the rest of my adult life. We got married. I no longer wanted my parents to live with me. That makes sense to you, does it not?

Friends change. The strengths and bonds of friendships change. This is normal, natural and expected. You had a wonderful friend for a long time, and now you are sharing her with someone else. You can choose, if indeed she is your friend, to rejoice in her new friendship with her boyfriend and wish them well. Perhaps someday you will be as fortunate and your friend will have new reason to celebrate with you. Rather than be upset about a friend finding a new friend, you can celebrate her good fortune.

Besides, possessiveness is not a positive quality of a healthy friendship. Choose to be excited and support your friend's new friendship. Show yourself what a fine adult you have become.

My best to you in your new life experience.

Doc

– – –

"When I moved to Florida from New York, my friend was so upset about the move she would not answer my phone calls to her from Florida."

When friends part company, rejection and jealousy often occur. Sometimes the friendships can withstand <u>distance</u> between friends, and sometimes not. That remains to be seen.

Often friendships contain some control issues. This means that you are my friend as long as you live up to my expectations. If I expect you will always live in my neighborhood, or you will always be my best friend no matter what, then I am bound to suffer some disappointment. Healthy friendship is not about control. Healthy friendship needs to include some celebration when something good and beneficial happens to you. I rejoice when you find a better place to live. I rejoice when your living conditions get better. I celebrate with you when life smiles upon you.

I stop speaking to you when I feel jealous and cannot control you any longer. That's not healthy for me, or for you.

You might <u>wait</u> to hear from your friend. Allow her to deal with <u>her</u> issues. If she is truly your friend, she will call you with a new understanding of your move. All change brings some stress with it. You can expect some each time you make changes in your life. Your friend is telling you that she is hurting. Give her time to heal and to decide where you fit in her life.

Your new city is also about <u>new</u> friends. Some friends from your old home town might prevail, but more than likely they will fade with time. Distance has a way of doing that.

Thinking about your note to me reminds me of a child's attitude, "I want what I want, when I want it! And, if I don't get it, I will throw a fit." Some adults are like that.

Enjoy your new home in Florida. I wish you some old friends and some new ones as well.

Peace,

Doc

— — —

"My boyfriend always criticizes me. He calls me lazy. Things he says cut me like a knife. He yells at me and hangs up on me on the phone. I don't know why I put up with his behavior for so long."

I don't know why you put up with him either. If what you are saying is true, you ought to drop him like a box of hot rocks! A friend ought to not be remembered for criticisms. No friend ought to yell at you, male or female. Friends don't hang up rudely while on the phone. A friend may indeed be politely critical of your behavior once in a while, but not "always critical." Friends do not say things that "cut like a knife." The man you are describing is <u>no</u> friend!

Counseling can be very helpful in sorting out issues like why you choose to date a man like you describe. Going to counseling is like going to college. In both instances you learn something new about yourself and you acquire ideas that were not available to you before. Counseling is education. I believe you need some new ideas about who you are and what you ought to put up with from others.

If I were you, I would consider some professional counseling. I would tell the counselor how your boyfriend treats you, and then say, "I don't know why I put up with his behavior." I think the professional you trust with this issue will be able to help. I think you ought to consider seeing someone very soon because I believe the man you call your friend is not in your best interest. I want <u>you</u> to believe it too.

Phone a counselor today, please.

Doc

— — —

"I want to give myself a chance, but I am not sure I deserve it."

Henry Ford said, "If you think you can't, you can't! If you think you can, <u>you can</u>!" I believe the same thing applies to the idea of "deserve." If you think you "deserve" something, then you deserve it!

My advice is to <u>start</u> thinking, "**I deserve a chance!**" You deserve a chance to be happy, peaceful, and calm. The choice is all yours. You deserve the right to work hard and achieve your goals. You deserve the chance to read, write and think daily and become more educated. This choice is yours for the taking.

You might whistle a happy tune while enjoying the thoughts, "I deserve lots of chances. I am a valuable, fallible human being and I deserve all the chances in life I can imagine. I am excited about my new attitude! I am a worthwhile human being. I am going to give myself the chances in life I want. Life is good! Wow! I feel better already!" Remember to smile. You <u>deserve</u> it also!!

Enjoy a better day,
Doc

— — —

FAKE IT...TILL YOU MAKE IT!

Once upon a time, I was involved with a special project where children were sent who were "too ill mentally" to ever be returned to their parents and families. The children in this particular hospital did not follow directions nor comply with the requests and expectations of their parents. They were thought to be "too ill to benefit from therapy." The plan was to house them in a safe environment where they could not harm themselves or their family members. They were to live in a hospital setting for the rest of their lives.

From time to time there were professionals who thought they could help the children and they received permission from the hospital administration and the parents to experiment. The doctors and the researchers sincerely wanted to disprove the theory that "these children were too mentally ill to ever be helped."

No one was ever really successful. The children continued to be almost totally uncooperative with their peers and with the adults who looked after them at the hospital. For example, if asked to sleep in their beds, the children would sleep under them, or in the bathroom, or in the hall. If asked to eat with a spoon, they would eat with their hands. If asked to urinate in the toilet, they would urinate everywhere but in the toilet. They seemed to work hard at being uncooperative.

One day a psychologist came to the hospital. He wanted to help the children and he believed he knew how. The psychologist received permission to "try it his way" for a while. He bought hundreds of red poker chips and he designed a very specific list of behavioral expectations for the children. He told the children that *if* they behaved as expected they could *earn* a red chip. He said that *if* they slept in their assigned beds at night, they would earn one chip. If they awoke in the morning when called they could earn another chip. If they got dressed before coming to breakfast in the morning they could earn another chip. If they ate with their spoon, instead of their hands, they could earn a chip. The children were *not* interested in this new game. They had no incentive to cooperate.

So, the psychologist took away the children's right to watch television. He took away their right to play in the yard. He took away their snacks and their desserts after dinner. He took away all their treats and their privileges. He took away all the activities the children liked.

He explained that from this point forward, the children would have to *earn* the privilege to do what *they* wanted by first doing what *he* expected. There was increased grumbling on the part of the children. They wanted what they wanted, when they wanted it! They were angry and upset when they didn't get what *they* wanted. We are all like that from time to time, I suppose.

It was not long before one of the children wanted a candy bar. It was explained that he could have the candy bar when he earned 2 red chips. The young boy had no chips. The doctor explained that he could earn one by eating his next meal with his spoon ... by sleeping in his bed tonight ... by taking a shower before he went to bed ... by not hitting another patient for the rest of the day. The young boy fussed, but he complied with the doctor's wishes long enough to earn 2 chips so that he could purchase the candy bar. The plan had begun to work!

It didn't happen overnight, but soon more and more children were doing what the adults expected in order to earn red chips to exchange for the things that they wanted at the hospital. More and more children began to act as directed. They began to act as their adult models expected. They began to behave as though they were not mentally ill. They stopped hitting and spitting on each other ... they slept in their own beds at night ... they urinated in toilets and not in the halls ... they took showers each day ... they agreed to dress in normally expected clothing for their day's activities ... they went to class when asked ... and they complained significantly less than before. Their behavior was changing!

There are always people who seemingly don't want others to be successful and there were those same people in this case. They said that the children were changing their behavior, but they weren't being cooperative because *they* wanted to be cooperative. They said that the children still wanted to misbehave even though they were "acting" cooperative. The skeptics charged the new psychologist with simply getting the children to "act normal." The doctor had his own belief: that it was acceptable if the children were only "acting" normal, because if they continued to "act" normal, they would someday grow to believe that this "acting" was indeed the right and personally acceptable way to behave. Someday the children would behave cooperatively because they believed that it was right and in their best interest to do so.

Within one year, some of the children were returned to their families. They were behaving, as a normal child would be expected to behave. Was it an "act" or not? There was much discussion on that topic.

Do you act cooperative because you *want* to, or because it is in your best interest, or because someone has raised you on red poker chips? You may answer those questions for yourself, if you like.

Let's move on. Not too long ago, administratively and clinically, I managed a chemical dependency treatment center for children between the ages of 12 and 18. By the time the children/druggies came to the Center for help they not only had a drug-abusing habit, they were very uncooperative with their parents, siblings, school personnel, religious leaders, law enforcement, and neighbors. Their lives seemed to be out of control and self-destructive, except to the young druggies themselves. They insisted, "They were doing what *they* wanted to be doing!" They said time and time again, "I want what I want when I want it!"

The behavior of the young druggies reminded me very much of the behavior of many of the children in the State Hospital. They were seemingly out of control … almost totally uncooperative … and demanding what *they* wanted when *they* wanted it.

The adolescents entered the drug program kicking and screaming. They "…didn't have a problem and they didn't want help!" Their message was clear. One young boy spit on his mother on the day of admission and told her he never wanted to see her again. He "...hoped she'd die, and soon!" One girl screamed at her mother, called her a "bitch" and said she'd kill her if she ever saw her again. The children were very abusive to their parents, even though there was usually no evidence that their parents had been abusive to them. How did the children get that way?

In some cases, the answers were simple. The boys and girls *practiced* a new set of behaviors or life-style until it became the acceptable life-style. They *acted* or *pretended to be* druggies, and eventually they made it!

I remember the first time I smoked a cigarette. My drama coach smoked when I was in high school and I wanted to be just like him. He smoked Camel cigarettes so I bought some. I lit one and inhaled deeply like he did. You're right! My eyes watered, I felt dizzy and nauseated, and coughed. I practiced in private so others would not see that I was not an accomplished smoker. I practiced and practiced and soon I could smoke and "be cool" like Mr. Jenkins. I had trained myself to be a smoker. I even trained my body to believe that it *needed* and *wanted* me to smoke on a regular basis.

It is possible for me to *drastically* change my behavior. I changed so very well from being a non-smoker to a smoker that several years later it was hard to give up the habit. I had to practice and practice, once again, to change back to a non-smoker. But, I did it and that is the point - I can change my behavior when I want to.

The boys and girls in the chemical dependency rehabilitation program changed their behavior also. Hundreds of angry, resentful, depressed, self-hating, uncooperative, snarling, biting, spitting, drug-abusing young people *reversed* their behaviors when they began to admit that their self-destructive acts were not in their own best interest. They were not self-destructive, angry, resentful, self-hating children when they were born. They *practiced* being that way! Adults did not make them that way.

You cannot be made to hate if you don't want to hate. That is the choice of each human being. We can choose to love or hate others, and ourselves. There are lots of choices about lots of things in the world.

Changing is not an easy process. Human beings cannot simply decide to be different and everything changes. First we have to admit that change would be in our own best interest. We have to have a reason to change. Many of us demand that *others* change so that *we* can feel better, rather than looking for ways in which *we* can make the situation or relationship more workable or pleasant ourselves. We tend to "point the finger" away from ourselves and toward someone or something external to ourselves.

I suggest that we look *within* ourselves to see what it is that "I" can do to help make this a better world in which to live, rather than blame others and wait for others to act first.

I met a young woman who looked sad and acted angry. I wanted to be her friend but she acted like she would rather not have me near her. In fact, she acted as if she would rather not have anyone relate to her. One day I asked her why she seldom smiled or acted friendly. She said something I will never forget … she said, "If I showed people my good side they will only take advantage of me!" She saw no reason to smile. How must she feel *inside*? I can only assume that she feels the same as she looks … sad and angry.

She found fault in others. She appeared to find little joy and happiness in life, and she sounded as if she thinks *other people* and *other things* are responsible for the way she feels. I'd like to tell her that she has options and choices. In fact, she has lots of options. I attempted to tell her that *if* she would relate in a friendly manner to me, I would very much like to be her friend. She was not impressed. She did not want to talk about that subject with me. She practiced being unhappy and angry for a long time and so she was skillful in producing these feelings for herself.

The young druggies that I treated were also well practiced in feeling miserable. They "felt like hell" most of the time and they blamed their boyfriends, girlfriends, mothers, fathers, brothers, sisters, teachers, ministers, and so on. But, sometimes, the young people would hear and understand. Something that we'd say or do would get through to them. They would actually begin to understand that *they* had choices about how *they felt* and about how others treated them. They thought adults didn't care about what happened to them. We'd tell them and show them that *we cared*. They thought and acted as if adults could not be trusted. We showed them that when we said something we meant it and we did what we said we'd do. They thought that all adults would like to get what they want. We told them the *facts*, to the best of our ability. They thought that adults are only out for themselves. We told them and showed them that we needed each other and that life is a team project. They began to trust us, work with us, and gain the insight that it matters what each of us does. They also grew to agree with me that it is fun and personally rewarding, to have a *friend* and to be *loved*.

If we are not emotionally disturbed or mentally ill, don't most of us want to have a real friend and to be loved? Of course we do! We want to fit in. We want the people around us to approve of us. We want to be loved.

The young druggies adopted a <u>miserable</u> set of attitudes regarding themselves and their lives. Then they lived them as though they were the only ones that could ever be followed. They said, "I behaved rotten, therefore I am rotten!" They made this statement with all the conviction they could muster. It was difficult to break through their armor and to introduce the notion of human fallibility.

Then came the idea that humans are somehow responsible for human emotion. We make <u>*ourselves*</u> happy or sad. I am the one who suffers the most from my unhappiness and anger. Therefore, I don't want to suffer anymore than I have to. It is my personal *choice* to be sad and miserable! I can *choose* to be happy, friendly, pleasant, kind, cooperative, peaceful, and gentle if I want to. Can't I?

My young druggie clients began to *choose* to be friendly, gentle, peaceful, cooperative, calm, and happy. They really did! The majority of them changed so drastically in a year and a half of treatment that their parents, ministers, grandparents, teachers and neighbors were amazed.

Human beings are *powerful* creatures! We can do great and wonderful things with our lives. We are capable of *change* whenever we decide to get *honest* with ourselves.

The first step the young people took is called *insight*. They learned some new information ... a light went on ... they took some friendly advice ... they thought about themselves and their plight honestly and objectively. They said, "Maybe, just maybe, Dr. Brown is accurate. Maybe I *am* responsible for my miserable life and the miserable way that I feel. Maybe if I did what he is suggesting ... maybe I could make a difference in my life ... just maybe."

Many of the teenagers liked the idea of living "one day at a time." Making an effort to change a personal behavior for a day was far less threatening than changing for the "rest of my life." One girl thought that even "a day" was too difficult a goal for her, so we made success even more possible to achieve. She said, "One moment at a time." She found success with this new attitude.

For these recovering druggies, the *intellectual insight* that "I am at least partially responsible for my sad state of affairs," was important for them to understand. Being responsible for my thinking and attitudes provides hope and gives a new sense of power because, it means, when I change *what* I *think,* my feelings and behavior will also change. I feel and act the way I do because of the *thoughts* I think.

The young woman in my story does not have to be angry, sad and miserable. She can learn to think differently. She now *thinks* that people will take advantage of her if she smiles, acts friendly, and is cooperative. She could *think* instead that people, like her mother, want very much to be her friend, enjoy a positive relationship with her, and enjoy her company. She *thinks* that it is unfair and awful that her father and mother got divorced and she cannot be happy without them the way they used to be. She could choose to *think* that the world is not always fair. She could think both her mother and father are happier apart than they were living with each other, and she could choose to enjoy their new happiness. She could choose to deal with the *present* rather than with the past, and enjoy the relative peace of the moment.

She does not have to feel miserable at this moment because she's not getting everything she'd like to have! She can ask herself the following question? What is it that I would have to tell myself *right now* to make myself feel better than I presently do? Then, she could tell herself, whatever is necessary, to get on with her happier life! Example? Life just doesn't always give me what I want. If life gives me a bag of lemons, I could choose to make some lemonade. Life seems to be spelled "HASSLE" from time to time. It isn't the hassle I *get that's important.* It's what I *do* with the hassle that's really important. Life can be one damn thing after another. Counting how many "damn things" I get is not as important as what I do about them and how I handle them. I have some choices, you know!

When life does not give her what she very much wants, she can *choose* to whine about it, or accept that "it" happened. It wasn't what she wanted, but she <u>can</u> stand it, and move on. Perhaps the supposed problem may even be a *window of opportunity* that cannot be seen clearly at the moment...

Human beings have *choices* about how they emotionally feel because they have *choices* about what they *think* about themselves and their environment. Humans feel the way they do because of the thoughts they think.

Most of the teenagers I worked with understood this insight eventually. They fought tooth and nail not to change ... they seemed to be willing to do almost anything to keep their misery, hatred, and resistance to change. They believed that *other* people and *other* things were responsible for their upset, period! Once they understood how <u>their</u> thinking and attitudes played a vital role in their emotional lives and how they behaved, they were willing to start making some changes. Once they saw that they were individually responsible for their miserable state, they started to agree, "We are not going to continue to punish ourselves as we had once learned to do."

These druggie children needed to care about themselves as individuals. They seemed to enjoy the new idea that they are VFHB's (valuable, fallible, human beings). They liked the way that new attitude felt.

They also had to believe they were worth the effort. They had to *like* themselves before they could start treating themselves well. The druggies treated themselves poorly because they hated themselves for the way they had behaved in their past. How else could they treat themselves as they did?

If the young lady in this story really liked *herself*, she would not alienate herself from her parents. She might even take some advice from them. She might even appreciate their efforts to befriend her. She might even invite her mother over for lunch and find out how good it feels to have a mother who loves her. It is amazing to me how human beings will work so very hard to keep loving people away from them.

This particular young woman has a mother who loves her dearly; who has remained her friend no matter what her daughter has done. The mother sends her support money; accompanied her to the delivery room when others were too afraid to go with her; makes sure that she has the items necessary to be a new mother; supplies clothing and furniture for the new baby; listens to her tears in the middle of the night when she calls on the phone; and is always available for requested support. However, it you were to watch when the mother does something kind for her daughter, you would see the daughter behave as though a stranger were doing something irritating to her. It seems to make no rational sense.

Why would a young woman, with a new baby, and no partner, push away a loving mother? It is a *learned*, self-defeating *attitude* that the girl has practiced for a long time. She learned to think about her mother as someone who does not have her best interest at heart. She was someone to avoid, someone to get around, and someone who was only there to stop her from having "fun." She practiced this thinking long enough to believe it. She got plenty of support from her friends because in some sub-cultures it is "popular" to find one's parents offensive.

What would ever motivate the girl to change? Her life is becoming more and more uncomfortable, unmanageable and painful. Her boyfriend, with whom she had a baby, wants her to "get out" of their apartment. He is "tired of the responsibility of caring for her and their baby."

Rather than get angry with the boyfriend at this point, let's concentrate on the less-fortunate young woman and the baby. She needs to survive somehow with her child. She needs to care enough about herself, which she has not done for several years. She needs to clean herself up, get help caring for the baby, and get a job to support the two of them. Will that be "easy?" No, but it is possible!

The first required change is in *attitude*. The young mother would do well to consider that she and her baby are worth the effort that she needs to make in order to save the two of them. She needs to *pretend* that they are worth the effort even if she does not really believe it. She probably will not believe it when she first thinks about it. She probably will not believe it when first she thinks the thought. She must *fake it ... till she makes it.*

"Fake It...Till You Make It," was one of our most popular and important phrases in drug treatment with the 400 children and families we served. It does not feel "right" to attempt something different than what you've been used to. Imagine the girl in the story calling her mother and saying, "I miss you and would love to visit with you. I am going to make a nice lunch for you this Thursday at noon. I'll clean my apartment, put on a pretty dress and a smile and make our time together a special one. Please join me." The mother and the daughter would both be uncomfortable and nervous because that is not typical behavior for either of them. But, it just might feel very good for both of them afterwards. I bet it would!

The first time we do something that we are unaccustomed to doing; we have to be somewhat uncomfortable. It is human and natural to feel that way. But, the more we *practice* being kind, appreciative, loving and gentle, the easier it becomes. Someone said that with practice we could do almost anything.

I have seen *practice* work "miracles" in the State Hospital with children, in intensive drug rehabs with adolescents and their parents, and in mental health centers with people of all ages. Human beings who were willing to *fake it ... till they make it*, made it!

What's the risk? What did the young woman in the story risk? She risks becoming less miserable ... gaining one or two close, trusted friends ... feeling calmer, more peaceful and more content. The risk is experiencing the world as an enjoyable place.

A person can start by repeating the following thoughts (again and again). And, while saying the words, like a great actor or actress might say them, *pretend* that *you really want to believe what you are saying.*

1. I am a valuable human being.
2. I am a fallible human being.
3. I deserve to be happy and healthy.
4. I am far more capable than I presently believe.
5. I am responsible for my happiness.
6. I want to be happier, calmer and more peaceful.
7. I am going to start today to *act* cooperative, appreciative, loving, kind and gentle, especially toward those who love me and care about me.
8. I am not too proud to ask for help.
9. I will keep *my* best interest in mind at all times.
10. I am going to *fake it, till I make it*, because *I am worth it!*

Food For Thought

- It is not uncommon to see a person behave in a certain manner and then say, "That's just the way I am ... I've always done it that way. There doesn't seem to be much I can do about it. It seems too uncomfortable, or phony, to act differently." They have a habit of behaving in a certain manner and believe they were born doing it that way. Have you ever said the very same thing to yourself? Were you aware that "faking it till you make it" is useful advice?
- Do you remember faking it till you made it? What were the circumstances?
- If this is a new idea for you, how might you put the idea to use in your life?

ANALYSIS OF ATTITUDES

"I am shy and quiet by nature. I would like to put this idea to use to help me overcome my shyness and lack of confidence in myself."

I believe you are "shy and quiet" by habit. It really does not matter how you got to where you are, the good news is, you <u>can</u> change.

First, you need to believe you have something to offer, something worthwhile to say to others. Perhaps you would be willing to accept <u>my</u> belief that <u>you</u> are a valuable human being with lots of interesting ideas to share with others. Look in your mirror and say, "Doc Brown believes in me! He says that I am a valuable, worthwhile human being. Doc Brown says that I have lots of interesting ideas to share with others. He says I cannot afford to be shy and quiet. Doc Brown wants to hear what I have to say, and he believes others do also." Be sure to <u>smile</u> at yourself while saying these words. Now, say them again, as though you <u>really</u> want to believe it. Practice this as many times as it takes you to believe it.

Also, set some not-so-shy-and-quiet goals for yourself. If you are taking college courses, plan on raising your hand at least once an hour and asking a question in class. This will seem uncomfortable at first, perhaps, but soon you will be enjoying your new, <u>comfortable</u> habit. Remember, you have something to share. You don't understand everything that happens in class, and you don't understand everything you read in your text. You have the right to ask questions and you have the right to learn from the answers. You are simply asking for the education for which you have already paid.

It's fun to share my ideas with you, especially when you share in return. Education, both in and outside the classroom, is a process of give-and-take. Think about doing both.

Thanks,
Doc

– – –

"There are ways I behave because I thought I was born that way. For example, I have social anxiety and have spent my life avoiding social

situations. I had very few friends in school and avoided public areas because I thought that was how I was supposed to be. It was just me. I want to be more social and outgoing!"

I agree with you. It can be enjoyable to be social and outgoing, and I wish both for you. I believe it <u>is</u> possible for you to become a more social person.

You were born with a brain that is comfortable in situations where you have <u>learned</u> to be comfortable. It's very normal to be a little uneasy in any new situation. Your brain has not yet learned how people are going to behave toward you. It does not know what your role is in the group. There are new faces to meet and greet. There can be some discomfort about the expectations of others.

But, the discomfort that you might feel is <u>natural</u>, <u>normal</u> and <u>expected</u>. In fact, there is a term to describe it. Cognitive dissonance is the feeling of discomfort that we experience when we attempt something new. So what? Well, we are designed to be a little uncomfortable in new situations until we learn our way around in the group. It means that we can <u>expect</u> an uncomfortable feeling when attempting something new, and that makes the feeling have less importance. It is something I am supposed to feel when in a new situation. Therefore, I don't have to run from the situation because I'm feeling a little uncomfortable. I'm OK.

For the most part, we are who we have <u>learned</u> to be. Make a plan for this weekend. Take a friend with you for some added support. Pick a place you would both like to visit. Go to a movie together. See a play. Go to the beach. Visit a local restaurant lounge and have a drink. Look around you. Notice other people being relaxed and having fun being together. Notice the good things happening around you. Look for evidence that <u>life is good</u>. You might notice you are not completely comfortable. That's not important to your new education. What is important is that you are out with a friend, enjoying life. Look for the <u>positive</u> aspects of the moment. "Hey, look at me! I am out with a friend, having a good time. Life is good and I am enjoying myself." A <u>positive</u> focus always feels better than the alternative. <u>Think</u> about it.

Rome was not built in a day. Your attitude is not going to change overnight. Small steps are easy to accomplish and <u>doable</u>. Take some small steps. Plan them. Look forward to them. Ease into a more sociable and outgoing perspective. Look for the positive progress you're making. Pat yourself on the back for your efforts. Life ought to be enjoyed. You can enjoy your life more everyday.

You have the potential to become the person you desire to become. Go for it, a step at a time …

Doc

— — —

"I want to learn to be positive and friendly toward other people in my life."

Great! Start now!! Start with the very next person you meet. Smile and greet them with a kind word. "Good morning, Mom. What a nice treat it is to see you this morning!" How's that for an example?

You can practice by looking in your bathroom mirror. Smile. A smile is hard to beat. It improves <u>your</u> feelings while giving the person you meet an opportunity to smile. I enjoy seeing a smile on the face of someone coming toward me. It makes me feel warm inside and always gives me a reason to smile back.

What this world needs is a positive and friendly atmosphere! We've gotten good at turning the spotlight on the negative. I think it's <u>wonderful</u> you want to be <u>positive</u> and <u>friendly</u>! What a lovely goal indeed. You will be more fun to be around and you will like yourself better in the process.

Sit down with a pencil and paper. Write down some friendly greetings. Write down what you are going to say the next time you see someone in your immediate family. Practice saying what you are designing on paper. <u>Act</u> friendly and kind. Pretend you are on stage, trying out for a part in a play. <u>Act</u> like the positive and friendly person you want to become. Think of a specific person and plan your greeting. Then seek her out. Use your new greeting with her, face to face. Watch her new reaction. Feel good about what you've done. Give her a chance to soak up your new-found excitement when seeing her.

It feels good to be close to people. It does not happen by accident. It takes someone, like you, to take the first step. "Positive and friendly" are great first steps.

Fake it, till you make it. Enjoy.

Doc

— — —

"The way I am is the way I have been brought up and I am not sure there is much I can do to change me."

Ok, you win. The way you are is the way you were brought up. Here you are. There are two possibilities the way I see it. Stay the way you are, <u>or</u> make an effort to change. Staying the way you are might be just fine. But, you just started college. That indicates to me that you don't want to stay the way you are. Indeed, you are reading, writing and thinking so as <u>not</u> to stay the same. You are <u>in</u> college, and at the same time saying, "I am not sure there is much I can do to change me." Have you thought about that?

In the first place, if you compare how you look today with a picture of you last year, or five years ago, it will be obvious that you are changing. Change is what we are about. Someone once said, "The only constant is change." You are changing. You react to your environment everyday and it shapes you, it changes you. "9/11" was a day that changed us all. You would certainly admit that. Events in our lives have the power to change us. And, **we have the power to change us.**

Here is a 3-step plan I am happy to share with you. When you want to change something about yourself, try this. First, you must decide there is something about yourself that is worth your time and energy to change. Example, "I don't like the fact that I smoke cigarettes!" Secondly, you must make the conscious decision that you are going to stop. "I not only do not like the fact that I smoke cigarettes, I have made the decision to STOP SMOKING TODAY!" Now you are well on your way to being a person with different behavior. Thirdly, you must <u>think</u> thoughts in <u>support</u> of your <u>new</u> desired behavior. Examples: "I am excited to be a non-smoker! I am no longer going to stink like an ashtray! My lungs are already healing from the damage I did to them! I am becoming a healthier human being! I am going to live longer as a non-smoker! I am proud of my ability to control what I put in my mouth! I have the strength, ability and willpower to be healthy! I am a non-smoker!"

There was a time when you didn't smoke. You didn't come out of your mother with the habit! You <u>learned</u> to smoke. You voluntarily <u>changed</u> from being a healthy human being to a smelly smoker. Now you can <u>change</u> back. We are such powerful people. We can do great and wonderful things. We can change from this to that, and back again.

If I think, "I can't change," I can't. If I think, "I <u>can</u> change," I <u>can</u>! It is not rocket science, it is <u>human</u> behavior. You can change, and so can I. We must <u>want to</u>.

Start today to <u>think</u> positively about yourself.

Doc

— — —

"I have the habit of being too aggressive and rude. People often complain about me. I've always found myself telling other people that this is just how I am and I cannot change."

It is a great excuse, isn't it! I'm mean, nasty and no fun to be around, and that's just how it is. Take it or leave it!

Ouch! I'd have to believe that someone who "often" gets feedback about being "rude and aggressive" has to also dislike himself. Do you imagine a healthy, well-adjusted person gets criticized for being rude and aggressive? I don't think so. When you were born, did people come to the hospital to see you and thought, "Wow, there is a rude, aggressive little kid!" I don't think so. You've learned to behave like this. You can certainly learn to behave differently once you decide that **you are worth it.**

I wonder what's behind your attitude. My guess is that you are angry about something. You must be angry at yourself. You push people away who would like to be close to you. What's that about? Healthy people want other people as friends, not enemies. Healthy people have little reason to be rude to others. If I like me, then I tend to like you. If I respect me, then I tend to respect you. If I don't like me, then I can easily not like you.

I can't change you, but **you can change you.** It would be a good idea for you to talk to someone about your behavior. Perhaps someone close to you, who thinks you are rude and aggressive, would be interested in helping you, if you gave him a chance. Perhaps there are family members who would love to give you some helpful feedback about how to change your rudeness into kindness. You'd have to be **interested** in listening to them, and **accepting** their feedback. You might learn some personally helpful information.

Often, the people around us have helpful ideas to share with us, but we push them away and don't give them a chance to be helpful. This might be one of those times for you.

There is always the possibility of seeking help from a college counselor, a counselor in the city where you live, a leader in your church or a relative you respect. There are many opportunities for help if you are sincere about wanting to change your behavior. The excuse that you have always been this way is not valid. It is just an excuse to continue to be the way you are.

I invite you to learn something about yourself and increase your personal joy in living at the same time. I wish you only the best.

Doc

– – –

"Perhaps I can use, "Fake it, till I make it," in order to get used to speaking up and expressing my thoughts to others. I will stop thinking, "This is the way I am," and accept the fact that I can change. Eventually I'll be less afraid to participate in conversations or debates instead of keeping thoughts and opinions to myself."

There is no "perhaps" about it. Imagining yourself "speaking up and expressing your thoughts to others" will increase the likelihood of your success. Making some paper-and-pencil notes will also help prepare you. Practicing your presentation in front of a mirror will help. Thinking the process through beforehand is the key.

You said it well when you wrote, "Eventually, I'll be less afraid to participate in conversations and debates." Take small steps, they are less scary. Take the opportunity to speak up in a conversation. Be proud of your effort. Think what you want to say before you say it. See yourself expressing yourself with confidence. Think, "I have something worthwhile to offer." Then, say it! Whether your idea is warmly received or not, feel good for expressing yourself. Expressing yourself is the goal. You don't need to be warmly received to have accomplished your goal. Your goal is to share yourself with others. That's your right <u>and</u> your responsibility. Go for it!

Doc

– – –

"I tried to quit smoking. I tried everything, including medicines and nicotine patches, but nothing was more powerful than my attitude. I blamed my friend, who was the first one to give me a cigarette. I wished I had never met him. Fortunately, I quit smoking six months ago when I said to myself, "I was not born smoking, and I can live once again without cigarettes. I know people with worse addictions than I who have quit. I can too!"

Well said! Thanks for sharing your progress and excitement with us. Stay healthy.

Doc

– – –

"It is my understanding that my anger has become more and more of an issue to those around me. I'd like to know how this story can benefit me."

"Fake It … Till You Make It" says <u>you</u> have <u>choices</u> about what you <u>think</u> and how you <u>behave</u>. Your anger is a <u>learned</u> habit which can be adjusted. You can decide that it is not healthy for you to remain angry any longer. You can learn to be a peaceful, well-adjusted person once again. You were not born this way.

You own your anger. It is yours. It is a part of you because **you give it a harbor in which to dock.** You can rid yourself of it when you choose to think that it is not serving any useful purpose. It is something like carrying around a bag of garbage. It stinks and makes you feel ill. It serves to make <u>you</u> feel badly. You likely share your anger with those around you and give them reason to dislike you. This hurts you even worse.

Anger is a form of <u>self</u>-hate. It is most abusive to the person carrying it. I bet you don't deserve to be angry. I bet you are punishing yourself because life has not treated you the way you want to be treated. "If life does not treat me the way I want to be treated, I will heap additional pain and suffering on me by making myself angry!" What sense does that make? Very little!

How can this story help you? In fact, the story can't help you. **You must help you!** Start by saying that you don't like the way you feel. "I don't like the results that my anger brings me! I don't like the way I feel inside, and I don't like the way others treat me when I behave as an angry man! I am willing to understand my anger and give it up!!"

What should I do next? I would ask for some help. Seek help from a professional counselor. Make a sincere effort to give up your anger and start enjoying life. You deserve it and you are worth the time and effort.

Just do it.

Doc

– – –

"I have attempted many times to get a college education but have not pursued it all the way because I lost confidence and went back to what felt comfortable."

So where would we be if we always retreated to where we are comfortable? We'd still be living in caves. It's <u>time</u> to get out of your "comfort-zone" to <u>risk a little</u>. You could risk becoming more intelligent by staying in college. You could take a risk by looking for a better job. Or, risk taking better care of yourself and your family. You could also risk spending more quality time with your family. And, you could risk becoming more in charge of your life.

I don't believe that you "lost" confidence. You didn't have it in the first place or you would have completed a college degree after the first admission. You need to build some confidence in yourself. How? Take a day at a time. Attend class. Read your texts. Complete your chapter notes and assignments. Read, write and think <u>everyday</u> about college-related material. Make college a part of your daily routine.

College is not hard. It just takes some discipline. Do you have discipline? Can you accomplish something you want to accomplish? Of course you can! Build a fire under yourself! Get motivated! Tell yourself, "This time, success is mine!" Mean it! Write it down. Write it a thousand times! Be a cheerleader for yourself.

College is a great place. It's where great minds go to learn even more. College is where men and women go to learn how to build bridges, sew arms and legs back on, fly to the moon, conquer disease, write great books, and love one another. College is where stupidity is put behind us. College is where we make lifelong friends. College is an exciting privilege.

College isn't for everyone. It's for those of us who truly want to understand, grow and make a difference. I invite <u>you</u> to come along.
Doc

– – –

"A great, new job opportunity presented itself. I applied for a job but came in second. I did not have the required college education. When the qualified candidate didn't work out, and I was her acting-assistant, I worked diligently to learn how to do her job even though I did not have a college degree. My enthusiasm and confidence got me the job! I didn't have the qualifications they initially wanted, but I faked it till I made it. It feels good to be successful!"

It feels good to read of your success! "My enthusiasm and confidence got me the job!" And so it is with life. I am once again reminded of what Dr. George Axtelle told me. He said, "The harder I work, the luckier I get!"

I imagine that in the not-too-distant future, you will also have earned a college degree. It sounds as though you and success are partners.

Congratulations!

Doc

— — —

"This story relates to my present position. I did not have 'secretary experience,' but I had a lot of law firm/office experience. So I just faked it. After two years of giving it my best shot I was asked to be a legal secretary in a newly-created legal department. I made it happen!"

Determination and enthusiasm can transport you to wonderful destinations. Help yourself! Enjoy your journey.

Doc

— — —

"Sometimes I have a hard time with my fiancé. To avoid any further upset I 'act' as though it is not a big deal with me. In a couple of minutes I forget about the conflict and go back to enjoying my time together with him. It works for me."

If it works for you, it can work for me. Thanks for the advice.

Doc

— — —

"I came from a pretty dysfunctional family, and I decided early in my school years that I wasn't good enough. I dropped out in the 9th grade. As the years passed I realized that I deserved better. I took the tests for the GED and passed them. I was intelligent enough to pass! It was then I knew I was a valuable human being and that I am far more capable than I believed."

What a wonderful difference it makes when we think **positive thoughts** about ourselves, our potential, and our abilities. The difference between being a valuable human being, or not, is an attitude. When I think, "I am," I am!

Once again, help yourself.

Doc

— — —

"I remember when I lost my best friend; my girlfriend. Losing both at the same time almost drowned me in pain. I felt so lost and betrayed. I felt people were my worst enemy. Everyone was out to get me and I was 100% alone. I decided after some grieving time to move on and become a healthier person. I convinced myself, despite my negative thoughts, that I am an important, wonderful human being and I am capable of loving and trusting again. I faked it for a while. I came out of it, wonderfully ahead."

When life gives us something other than what we want, we can become very upset. We not only grieve the loss of a friend, we may choose to get angry at everyone. "If I cannot have the one friend I want, and have her forever, I will dislike all people! I will show everyone how <u>very</u> miserable I can be when I don't get what I want!"

Children behave in the same manner. "I want what I want, when I want it! And, if I don't get it, I will raise holy hell!" I'm not sure where they learn the routine, but they are good at it. Many of us carry the same behavior into adulthood.

It's not a fun experience to lose someone you love. But, like you said, after some grieving, you convinced yourself you are capable of loving and trusting again." <u>And</u>, I believe it is still better to have loved and lost, than never to have loved at all.

Enjoy.

Doc

— — —

"Since I am the only child of four to graduate from high school, I never thought I would be able to perform at the college level."

Since you are the only child of four to graduate from high school, you are the <u>most likely</u> to also graduate from college. <u>Think</u> about it.

Enjoy your college classes. They may turn out to be the best years of your life.

Doc

— — —

"I had hit rock bottom with 3 beautiful little girls. I was not sure what to do or where to go. My husband was an abusive alcoholic. I cried myself to sleep each night and spent my lunch hours crying in my car and feeling sorry for myself and my girls. One day I looked at my girls and thought, "They see me weak, they watch me give up and see me give in." I stopped crying, stood up for myself, and fought back for the things I believe in. As the days went by I did get stronger. I sure had to fake it sometimes though. Now, five years later, I am remarried to a wonderful man. I am happier than I have ever been, and everyday I watch my girls become healthier."

You stopped crying. You stood up. You fought for the things you believe in. You got stronger. You decided you and your girls were worth the effort. You made a new life for the 4 of you. Today, you are "happier than you've ever been." I applaud your energy and enthusiasm. I encourage you to continue to take VERY GOOD care of yourself. My very best to you!

Doc

— — —

"I have thought many unhealthy things about myself. I believe I am not good enough for certain people. I believe I am better than others. I am not good enough as a parent. I am unemployable. I haven't felt worthy enough to expect better. I want to feel worthy of being loved, worthy of being educated, worthy of being looked up to and cherished. I want to be proud of myself. I plan on putting the idea of "Fake it till I make it" to use by acting like a smart, eager,

responsible, compassionate mother, girlfriend, student, daughter and friend."

Wow! What a beautiful transition in attitude! You clearly demonstrate both the negative and positive attitudinal choices available to each of us. And, what a wonderful difference a change in attitude makes.

Dr. Albert Ellis defines us as <u>fallible</u> human beings (FHB's). We are all the same in that regard. I added a "V" to his definition. I believe we are valuable, fallible human beings. We are valuable because we are alive and full of potential. I accept the idea without argument. I am a VFHB and so are you.

Therefore, **you are "good enough."** You are not better than some people, and no worse than others. As a living, breathing human being, you are employable. You become employable by desiring to be. You are automatically "worthy" because you <u>think</u> you are. You are certainly worthy of being loved when you decide to love yourself. You are worthy of an education when you decide to visit your local public library. Education is your right. It is yours for the taking. Others will look up to you and cherish you when you respect yourself.

When you like and respect yourself, your goals of friendship and respect from others will follow. You will become a magnet for others who like and respect themselves.

Personal pride and an increase in self-esteem will certainly be yours when you behave as an eager, responsible and compassionate mother, daughter and friend. Helping others is a wonderful way to feel good inside.

I highly value your decision to construct new and <u>positive</u> attitudes for yourself. Positive attitudes are a highly combustible fuel for your new engine. They will make you operate better than ever. They are free for the taking. Design them with respect for yourself and your children.

I am proud to know you!

Doc

— — —

"I have bad habits that my mom and others wish to change, but I always tell them I can't change the way I am. I was born like that!"

If indeed you have bad habits that you and others wish you'd change, then you better <u>change your attitude</u> about where they came from. Your bad habits are <u>learned behaviors</u>; you were <u>not</u> born with them. You <u>are</u> trainable. Your habits can be changed.

If your mom and other people are suggesting you change some of your habits because they are <u>not</u> in your own best interest, then I suggest you take their feedback seriously. Often, family and friends have insights that can be very valuable.

In this case, <u>you</u> agree your habits need some modification. You seem to be hiding behind the idea that <u>your</u> bad habits are beyond your control. I believe you know better, you just don't want to make the effort to change.

I also believe you'd like yourself better when you make the effort to change. It seems obvious that your mother and your friends would.

Fake it, till you make it. You're worth the effort!

Doc

— — —

"I rarely ask anyone for help because of my pride. I've always been that way. I am going to use this strategy to get the help I need, whatever it may be."

Would you recommend that when a man is hit by a car, and the EMTs arrive, he ought to say, "No thanks, I don't need your help, I can do it myself?" Of course not!

We need each other. We go to the dentist because we choose not to repair our own teeth. Ha! We take our cars to garage because we can't do all the repairs ourselves. We ask for tutorial help in college because some courses are extra difficult. We have others build our homes because we don't have the time and skills required to do the job ourselves. Asking for **help** makes good sense.

Pride is sometimes a destructive attitude. It keeps us from being successful. When your attitude keeps you from getting the help you need, then it is self-defeating. I am very pleased to read that you are starting to ask for help when needed. Smart thinking!

Doc

— — —

"IF YOU DO, WHAT YOU'VE ALWAYS DONE, YOU'LL GET WHAT YOU'VE ALWAYS GOT"

It was the day before Easter, and once again this year my wife was in the kitchen preparing an Easter ham for family and friends who were to have dinner with us on Easter. The house was filled with the aroma of good things cooking.

And like always, I wandered through the kitchen to see what "help" I could be in the process. I stood for a moment watching my wife cut the ends off the ham that was being prepared to meet the heat of the oven. She carefully cut through the ham bone and carefully cut a slice, several inches think, off both ends of the ham. I was not surprised for I had seen this process before. For some reason, this time I was more than curious. I asked my wife why she cut the ends off the ham. I didn't want to be critical of the process, for the outcome was not to be criticized! I simply wondered what removing the ends of the ham did in helping the ham cook to its' delicious conclusion.

I explained that I was not being critical. I simply wanted to know the reason for removing the ends of the ham? She explained, "This is the way my mother taught me to do it. I have always done it this way." I could attest to that fact myself. I could not argue with her logic.

The next day my mother-in-law came to dinner. When the conversation settled down a bit, I asked her if she cut the ends off her Easter ham when preparing it to be cooked. She said, "I have always done that, yes indeed." I asked if there was a particular reason why she did that. She said that there was a very good reason indeed. "My mother taught me to do it that way!"

It seemed that she did not know of a special culinary reason for the operation, other than her mother's habit of doing it.

So now my curiosity was piqued! I had to search out my mother-in-law's mother and ask her. This was accomplished some weeks later when we went to visit with her for an afternoon. I asked her to explain her personal recipe for preparing an Easter ham.

She told a very interesting story. She said that Grandpa, her husband, was a very paranoid man when it came to butchers and butcher shops. He would not allow Grandma to go to the butcher shop alone, because, "Butchers have a tendency to cheat woman and sell them less expensive cuts of meat than what they ask for. They are clever at it and it takes another man to beat them at their own game! So, I would tell Grandpa what I wanted from the butcher shop and he would always shop for me. But, Grandpa would always try to 'treat me' by buying cuts of meat that were larger than what I had asked for. This seemed to be his way of telling me that he loved me. When he shopped for me at Christmas, he would buy me a 25-pound turkey rather than the 15 to 20-turkey I requested. And, on Easter, he would buy me the largest ham he could find in the butcher shop. The hams were so large that they would not fit in my baking pan and I would always have to cut the ends off to get them to fit."

It seems that the practice of removing the ends of the ham carried on for three generations regardless of the size of the hams or the size of the pans.

Food For Thought

- "Old habits die hard," someone said, but they <u>can</u> indeed die. They can be modified by a change in our thinking. What habits have <u>you</u> changed? How did you do it? What did you think differently?
- Is there something you or your family has done for generations that "the story of the ham" brings to mind? Would you share your story, please?

ANALYSIS OF ATTITUDES

<u>Changes I've Made:</u>

"I have recently taught myself to calm down almost immediately after getting upset. This book has made me realize that I am in control of myself and my emotions. I tell myself to 'step back and relax.' I sit down for 5 minutes and then go back to work. I have been very successful with this new routine."

The proof is in the pudding. Knowing we have some **control** is enough to make a positive difference in our lives. It does not take years of professional therapy to understand some simple facts about how our emotions work. **We feel the way we do because of the thoughts we think.** When we change our thinking, our feelings automatically change. Taking a few moments in 'time-out' can do the trick. A few deep breaths also help.

Thanks for sharing your success.

Doc

— — —

"I used to cut myself down. I would tell myself I was ugly, fat and not smart enough. I finally realized that my life is great and stopped belittling myself. I am beautiful. I am not fat. I was recently admitted to college which means I must be smart. I changed by talking to myself in respectful ways. I decided I <u>deserve</u> the many good things in life that I have. I realized that if I continued to be so critical of myself, I would not be able to achieve my goals. It is working!"

There are two steps to follow in order to achieve a goal. The first is to **act** in the direction of your goal. **Act** like the person you want to become. Secondly, **think** in a manner that **supports** your new goal. If you want to be **successful** in a college class, **act** as you think a successful college student would act, and **think** in positive ways to support your new behavior.

Act: Attend class; arrive early; sit in the front; bring your books, notebooks and a pen to every class; read, write and think about the course subject matter at least 5 days each week; act interested in the class; ask questions; participate in class discussions; and wear a smile. **Think positive thoughts:** "This course is doable. This is a dream come true. I am proud to be a college student and to be achieving such an important goal in my life. I am improving my life. I am on my way to becoming a college graduate. I will take one day at a time and give it my best shot. I can do this!"

Now that you have stopped cutting yourself down, you are free to enjoy new and exciting successes. Congratulations to you!

Doc

– – –

"Early in high school I started to go to parties. I went to every party I could find. I would get drunk at parties and when I was bored. Anytime I could drink I would. My friends thought it was fun to get drunk all the time. I moved to Florida two months ago. I stopped drinking and I stopped going to parties. I got a job and started attending International College."

It is very likely that your move to Florida and your new respect for yourself has **saved your life!** Remember how you used to behave versus how you behave today. Life **without** alcohol is an exciting improvement. Continue to respect yourself. Employment and attendance in college beats drunkenness any day of the week! Look for new peers who are positive examples of where you want to be. Enjoy your new life. Congratulations!

Doc

– – –

"My uncle is close to death from cancer. I can't control or change the situation. All I can do is hope he is comfortable until he goes. Instead of being upset and stressing about something over which I have no control, I am dealing with it one day at a time."

We usually don't discuss "death" until it gives us little or no choice. Your uncle has brought the subject into your life and you are therefore forced to deal with the idea. I empathize with your family. And, I applaud your attitude. "I can't control the situation," so rather than pretend the situation is different than it is, I am dealing with what happens, one day at a time.

So often we deny reality and, in our heads, make the situation more difficult and painful than required. Death is a natural consequence of life. Everything that lives will die. Death can be a peaceful end to a great deal of suffering. Some folks believe life is hell and death is something to be celebrated. **Our thinking makes it so**. I was taught many years ago that our perceptions create a different "reality" for each of us. "Perceived reality" is what we experience.

I wish your uncle was not suffering. I wish he could be with you forever. I wish he and you had no disappointments in your lives. I wish you could have anything and everything you desire. These wishes lead to pain and suffering. I like your attitude! It seems much healthier.

I wish you continued peace.

Doc

— — —

"One of my habits was to leave my dirty dishes in the sink for my mom to wash. I decided that's not fair to her. Now I wash my dishes right away after I am done eating. I also wash whatever else is in the sink. My mom works hard. I need to do things for myself!"

One reason I like the idea of "family" is that the members work **together** to help and support one another. It beats coming into the world and having to make it on our own. Were that the case, none of us would survive. Human babies are helpless creatures. They would soon die were it not for adults to care for them. The family unit makes good sense from the moment of birth. To put it simply, we **need** each other.

As children, we are dependent. We look to our parents for love and support. We expect they will meet all our needs, and then some. We can develop into pretty selfish little critters. Moms and dads have been trying to teach their children to clean their rooms, put their toys away, and generally clean up after themselves. Sometimes this training can take years and years before it catches on. Ha! "I think the world revolves around me and that parents are on this planet to serve me." Such is not the case.

Perhaps the "age of enlightenment" comes when children understand the responsibility of parenthood and make a personal effort to indeed become a real, working, cooperative part of the family unit. Those are special moments in the hearts of parents! "Wow! My son thinks enough of me to chip in around the house! Apparently, my persistence and dedication have been worth it. Wonderful!"

Don't stop now. Go for it! There's lots of cooperative work to be done in your family. The good news is your efforts increase smiles, appreciation, respect and love.

Doc

— — —

"I used to not participate in class. I used to sit in the back of the class. I did this so I would not be called on by the teacher. I was always afraid I would give the wrong answer. I was also afraid that other students would make fun of me. I just came to class, did my class work, and handed in my homework. That's all changed now! I attend class and ask questions. I participate. If I don't understand, I ask for help. I'm not afraid to ask for help anymore. I've learned that I can stand in front of the class and read my chapter notes out loud without feeling scared. The more I participate, the more I learn. The more questions I ask, the more I understand. I can accomplish what life throws at me. I am successful when I make an effort."

I teach because I enjoy students like you! I work hardest when you do. I am motivated by your enthusiasm. Your questions challenge me and make teaching fun. Education is a participatory process. When you behave as though you want to learn and allow me to be your mentor, I come home after class at night and have trouble falling asleep. Education is exciting! It makes the world go around. It sure beats the alternative … stupidity.

Welcome to college. Your new attitude is very impressive indeed!

Doc

— — —

"A habit I've changed regards my note-taking. I have learned when I truly pay attention and understand the main ideas my notes are clearer and aid my comprehension."

Research indicates that if you are a motivated listener, you tend to remember **half** of what you **hear** in a lecture at the end of an hour. One day later it is expected that you will remember **half of the half**, or **25%** of what you heard in the lecture. Your retention is poor unless you do something additional to assist it.

Research also indicates when you **read** for an hour, you are likely to remember **half** of what you read a day later. Therefore it seems reading is **twice** as effective as listening.

Taking **notes** while listening, and **reviewing** your notes several times, fortifies comprehension. Being successful in college depends on taking quality notes and reviewing them with **interest**.

You've learned a valuable lesson.

Doc

— — —

"In high school, all I did was study. I didn't even go out with friends on weekends. As I've grown up, I've learned to better manage my time. Now I have discipline as well as fun. As a result I have better relationships with people around me. I am a happier person."

I remember attending graduate school and being told by one of my professors, "Man's purpose on earth is the acquisition of knowledge." Perhaps he meant that to be a "primary purpose," but surely not the "only" purpose.

Life is to be **enjoyed**. We spend a short time on this planet and we ought to find something **everyday** to enjoy. Learning can be fun and enjoyable, but so can a day at the beach. It seems to me that both are a defensible part of life.

I am pleased you've found both. Enjoy.

Doc

— — —

"A habit I learned long ago was complaining about everything. I didn't realize I was doing it until my boyfriend pointed it out. I started to listen to what I was saying. I was shocked! I was a negative person. I now make a conscious effort to <u>think positive</u> before I speak. When my thoughts are negative, I change them before speaking. It makes a wonderful difference in my life."

"I started to listen to what I was saying." What a wonderful idea! Thinking before you speak makes a world of difference. Positive thinking helps create a positive person. It means you will be living with someone more enjoyable. That idea makes me smile! Congratulations to you! Enjoy …

Doc

— — —

"This story made me look back and think of the people that are gone from my family and think of all the people I wish I had taken the time and interest to learn from."

I understand. With the ever increasing emphasis on living in the fast lane, I am concerned that many folks will have the same longing. The opportunity to show interest and learn from those close to you is not past. Take time to smell the roses. Talk to those you love and respect. Ask about their lives and experiences. Your seniors have a great deal to offer you in both experience and wisdom. Asking relatives to write down their most memorable experiences and lessons learned can be a treasure you will cherish.

Instead of having remorse for what didn't occur in your past, make <u>this</u> moment count? I believe you will be pleased you did.

Doc

\- \- \-

"I started smoking cigarettes when I was eleven years old. It was a habit I picked up from watching my father smoke. As an adult, I got bronchitis. I thought about my life <u>and</u> about death. I decided I wanted to live. I've stopped smoking!"

You chose **<u>life</u>**. I'm proud of you!!

Doc

\- \- \-

"I've had the habit of telling 'little white lies.' The thing about it is they never stayed 'little white lies.' They've always turned into BIG, LONG, CONFUSING LIES. I have hurt a lot of people in the process. I recently realized that the pain that comes from telling a lie is much worse than telling the truth. A huge burden is lifted every time I tell the truth. Telling the truth has not come easily. I am still working to change. I feel <u>much</u> better about myself now."

Life is an education. We make mistakes, but we can <u>learn</u> from them. You apparently suffered from self-imposed pain by telling lies. Your pain gave you a reason to think about what you were doing and you changed your behavior. We learn to do some self-defeating things in our lives, but **<u>we can change</u>**. That's a beautiful part of being human.

Thanks for sharing your change with all of us.

Doc

\- \- \-

"I have changed my habit of worrying about my physical appearance. I used to spend hours applying makeup before going out in public. I felt naked without it. I decided that I am a beautiful person and I don't need all that paint on my face anymore. I also care less about

what others think of my appearance. I am a happier person because of my change in attitude."

Congratulations to you! I really like the idea that you are a **beautiful person** without a painted face. How nice it would be if more of us thought the very same way.

Doc

– – –

"I changed the way I raise my children. I am not raising my children the way I was. I talk to my children everyday. I sit down to eat with my children. They are allowed to come into my bedroom and sit on the bed and talk with me for as long as they choose. I was not allowed into my parents' room. It was off limits. Conversations with my mother were always 'safe.' We did not discuss unsafe topics. I tell my children they may discuss anything with me, no matter what it is. I will always love them. I never let my kids think I expect them to be perfect."

Family members need each other. Children need parents to share their joys <u>and</u> sorrows. You make your children feel **welcome** in your life. I applaud you for that! You create opportunities to enjoy your children everyday, and you give them opportunities to be close to you and learn from you. Congratulations to you and to your family!

Doc

– – –

"My response to, "How are you today?" has changed. In the past, my response was, "Fair to medium." I believe it's a response to the height of a tobacco crop and I've never farmed tobacco. After reading <u>The Pocket Therapist</u> when someone asks me how I am, I always have a super positive response. I even put a very positive message on my answering machine. "It's a great day! I can't wait for tomorrow to arrive because I get better everyday." I'm not just thinking differently, I am thinking positively!"

We feel the way we do because of the thoughts we think. When we change our thinking, our feelings automatically change. You started thinking **positive** thoughts and you started to feel happier. It's not hard to understand. It just takes a **change of attitude**. Dr. Maxie Maultsby, Jr. once wrote, **Help Yourself to Happiness**. **It's there for the taking.**"

Doc

– – –

"I decided to change my thinking habits! I decided I am <u>worthy</u> of a good man. I have always dated losers. I didn't think I deserved a man with good manners, a drive to succeed, and one who dressed well. Last weekend my boyfriend came home drunk, like he's been doing for 3 months. Instead of threatening, yelling and crying, I helped him pack his things. He is gone! I will not let my old thoughts back in to control me. I deserve a good life and someone respectful to share it with. I will not settle for less anymore. I am a great person with a great personality and sense of humor. I see my life differently now. I am excited about applying more positive thoughts and actions to improve my life. My new journey has just begun. I am taking control of my life! Now I believe in me. I understand my life is what I make it. I can choose what side to see it from."

It seems to me that heaven and hell are right here on earth! You chose to get out of hell with a new and positive **respect for yourself**. I congratulate you on your new positive attitude. The difference between being a worthy or not-so-worthy human being is all in your head. A basic **attitude of worthiness** makes good sense. Nothing good comes from an attitude of unworthiness.

You are worthy of loving yourself. **You are worthy** of loving someone else. **You are worthy** of making the effort to find someone who will love and respect you in return. I believe the more you love yourself, the more you will insist on a relationship with someone who loves you. Settle for nothing less.

I am convinced you are now on a path that is more in your best interest. Thanks for sharing your journey.

Doc

— — —

"I have been able to change habits. Last September I bought a new car. Right then and there I made the decision <u>not</u> to smoke in my car."

I drive to and from the college everyday watching young men and women with their arms hanging out of their car windows, cigarettes in hand. Their habits **stink** too badly to have them **in** their cars. Their cars don't smell badly, but their bodies do. Their bodies **stink**, inside and out. What about their lungs and other organs? Oh well, it does not matter, no one can see them!

I agree. Save the cars and the hell with our bodies! Huh???

Doc

— — —

<u>Family Traditions:</u>

"My father used to mix rum with hot tea and drink it when he had a cold. He would mix enough and drink enough to get drunk. Once when I had a cold, my father gave me his "special drink." It didn't make me feel better, I just got drunk. I asked him why he drinks rum in his tea. He said his father did it. He learned from him. I think that every time he has a cold it is just an excuse to get drunk. I am choosing not to follow in his footsteps."

Your caution is admirable. There are many excuses for abusing drugs and having a cold appears to be one of them. I remember a grandfather who used to put a shot of bourbon in tea when he was ill. He only did that "once in a while." In any case, I believe your choice is in your own best interest.

— — —

"We have a tradition in our family regarding the order in which we eat our food. When I was growing up I was taught to always eat my vegetables first, and the meat last. It has stuck with me to this day. I won't even touch the meat portion of my meal until all my vegetables are gone. I think it is healthy that way."

The order in which you eat your food may or not matter. What you eat certainly does. It appears you are <u>thinking</u> about your food intake and that matters. Enjoy.

— — —

"We always put up our Christmas Tree in November."

Several years ago I was anxious for the holidays to roll around. I started to put up our tree on Halloween night. A group of little people came to our door to ask for treats and one of them saw the tree which only had the lights on it at that point. He asked what it was. I told him it was a "Halloween Tree." He immediately ran back down the driveway shouting, "Look Daddy! The man has a Halloween Tree!"

A fellow professor spent his life in the Navy. He was not able to be with his family in December. They decorated their Christmas tree on the first of every July in Saint Thomas and the family came there to celebrate.

Maybe we all ought to do what makes sense to us and our families.

— — —

"We've had a tradition in our family as long as I have been alive. We all get together to decorate a Christmas tree. Even though I am married now and have a home of our own, we all go to mom's house to decorate her tree. It isn't as unique a story as you cooking a ham, but it is something we all love to do."

There ought to be special times each and every year, and you have created one for your family. Yours sounds very special indeed.

— — —

"Every New Year's Eve, my family and I leave our house just before midnight. We make sure we are all out of the house before the New Year starts. We take a walk around the block and then all return home. We have done this for as long as I can remember. I asked my grandmother way we did this. She said her parents did the same thing. It brings new luck into the house every year. You know, it seems to work!"

I have to agree with you. If it seems to work, stay with the program! It sounds like a loving and fun family tradition.

— — —

"Every Christmas Eve my family gathers at my Grandma's house. We eat a large dinner. After dinner everyone goes for a walk with the exception of my grandma and my uncle. The purpose of the walk is to listen for Santa's Sleigh Bells. The truth is that my uncle stays behind to ring the bells, and grandma stays behind to wash the dishes. Even though most of us know the truth by now, we still enjoy the walk, and the sound of the sleigh bells ringing."

I think the "truth" is the bells you hear are really Santa's sleigh bells! Your uncle is just trying to pump up his self-esteem. Ho, ho, ho!

— — —

"It is a tradition in our family to make meatballs for every holiday celebration. One year, a long time ago, my grandma accidentally put a jar of grape jelly in with the sauce while she was cooking. She said she was so busy she did not notice what she had done. When she served the meatballs we all thought they were the best ever. She did not understand why they turned out sweet rather than spicy. She saw the empty jelly jar and started to cry. Since then, every holiday, we 'accidentally' put grape jelly in the meatball sauce."

Perhaps that's how great recipes are created. Sounds delicious! Thanks for sharing.

Doc

— — —

STINKY

It was a cold, dark, winter's day in Indiana. The lobby of the mental health center was filled with patients waiting to be helped. They were people in need of many things. They lacked coping skills; they lacked meaning in their lives; they lacked understanding; and they hurt.

Among the adults sat a young lad of ten years. His aunt was a patient at the center and had come there on a weekly basis for the past three years. She had a need she believed was being met by her therapist, and she continued to come for treatment. She believed she was being helped, and she wanted the same compassionate treatment for her nephew. She saw much of herself in the young man and was afraid for him; she didn't want him to go through what she had experienced in her young life. She cared about him and his future and wanted to help end his hurt before it got worse. She had seen the adults in her life as people who did not understand, and she now wanted to present herself to her nephew as someone who understood. She understood better than most, and she brought the young man to her doctor for advice and help.

"Stinky," as the boy was called, was afraid. He had lost 28 pounds recently, pounds that he could not afford. The laughter of youth was gone from his face. He was so very serious. He was shaking, not only on the inside like so many adults, but also on the outside where it could be noticed and not easily ignored. His face gave evidence of anxiety. He was not enjoying the heritage of his age, but was dealing with problems with which he could not cope. He was suffering and his aunt knew it. She brought him to see her therapist against his mother's wishes. She remembered that as a child she had begged for help and no one had listened. She told of the endless hours and days when she was alone with her thoughts and had no sympathetic listeners to share them. She well remembered her hurt and she wanted help for her young friend, help that she had not been able to find until late in life.

She begged, "Please help Stinky. He needs someone to talk to and confide in, someone who will listen and not punish him for his fears. He feels very much alone. I have tried to help him, but I just hurt with him and I'm not able to help. I cannot find the words necessary to change his beliefs. He knows that I care about him and yet I am not able to help ease the pain. You must help Stinky and me! Please!"

What must be done? It was evident that this young man was in need of help. He reminded the mental health professional of a milk shake machine in the old Dairy Dell where he enjoyed milk shakes as a boy. There was no doubt that something was being stirred up. The little boy shook and he looked at the therapist and said, "I'm, scared. I can't sleep at night. I throw up my food and my mother is mad at me. When I'm afraid, my mother and grandmother send me to my bedroom and tell me to stay there till I'm better and then I may come out of my room. They don't understand that I'm scared."

The therapist invited the boy into his office and asked him what was wrong. Stinky said that he had been going to church for the past two months at his mother's request and that was the beginning of his problems. He said the preacher told the children that they must not sin. They were not to be bad, and they were not to make mistakes or the punishment would be something that they would never forget. Stinky told the therapist of an evil thing that lived beneath the ground. It watched for boys and girls who made mistakes and did bad things. It could, and would, reach up out of the earth and grab them and pull them down into the fiery depths of the earth, never to be seen again. It was a bad thing! It was called "the devil" and it lurked in the shadows waiting for young boys and girls to be bad, and took them home with him. Stinky had never seen this devil but he *believed* that it existed and he was afraid of it.

Stinky remembered no sermons about the "love of God" or "the understanding of adults," but he remembered clearly the presence of the devil. He was afraid to go to school and he was afraid to play with his friends. It was not very hard to be bad and therefore it would not be very hard to be pulled into the center of the earth by that bad thing that was constantly after him. He had to always be on his guard and that was not fun. He was very, very frightened!

Stinky had heard adults speak of this creature. He didn't want to be hurt, and he didn't want to spend the rest of eternity in the center of the earth with the creature either. He shook! He cried!

The therapist told him that there are adults who know of no other way to get little people to behave than by scaring them. He told Stinky that when he was a little boy, there was a "boogie man." The Boogie Man worked for the sanitation department and rode the garbage truck every week and collected the garbage in the city. He was the same person who took bad little girls and boys with him when he came around to collect the garbage. But there was something wrong with that story. The therapist knew plenty of little boys and girls who did things that were "wrong," and the Boogie Man never picked them up. They were still on the block. They stole candy from the corner grocery and lied to their parents and cheated on tests in school and the Boogie Man never came to get them. It was all a fairy tale. It was the way the adults tried to get kids to do what THEY wanted. There was no Boogie Man. There *were* parents who could punish their children. There were teachers who could punish them for misbehaving. There were police who were paid to catch bank robbers. There were jails to hold the criminals, but there was NO Boogie Man! He was just a make-believe character who was invented to frighten children to keep them in line.

Stinky smiled. He must have understood. He said, "I see what you mean! But, all the big people where I go to church believe in the devil, and they can't all be wrong. Maybe the devil *is* real and the Boogie Man is *not* real.

Stinky's new confidant told him of the time when thousands of Spaniards believed that the world was flat. They would not travel too far from home because they believed that they would fall off the world and never come home again. They were afraid. They knew that the world was flat, and they were afraid to travel to the edge.

Stinky said that he had heard that story in school. He said he knew that the world was round, even though so many believed it to be flat. The therapist told Stinky that if all those people could be wrong about the shape of the world, then so could all the big people that he knew be wrong about the devil. It was a story that people made up to control the behavior of others. If you can convince people to be afraid of something, then you can control their behavior. If you want people to stay around home, then you tell them that the world is flat and they will fall off and never come back if they go too far from home. No one wants to fall off the world and never come back, so they will stay home and not travel too far even when they are not being watched. It works, and Stinky could begin to see the point.

This was not enough though, for now Stinky was afraid for the therapist. He said, "You had better be careful too or the devil might hear you talk this way about him, and he might come and get you too!" At this point, the therapist became aggressive. He said, "If you learn where the devil is and how to get a message to him, tell him to come to see me. I'll be happy to scold him for scaring a nice little boy like you. Just tell him where I am and that I'm waiting to meet him whenever he's ready!" Stinky smiled but did not reply.

The day continued and the therapist spent an hour with Stinky's aunt in therapy while he waited in the lobby. It was not to be known for a couple of weeks, but Stinky met a nice lady in the waiting room who asked him why he was visiting the mental health center. He told the lady of his fear of the creature that lived under the soil and of his talk with the doctor down the hall. He told the lady how the doctor did not believe in the devil and how he challenged the devil to come to see him and that he doctor would punch him in the nose for scaring the little boy.

That next week, the lady from the waiting room went to see the preacher and told him how the therapist did not believe in the devil and how he had told the little boy in the waiting room that there was no such thing. The preacher told the woman that he could understand, for "all psychologists are atheists." The woman came back to see the therapist for further treatment and told him what she had told the preacher and what he had said about therapists. She said what she told him must have upset him, for the very next Sunday, the preacher gave a sermon on how his people will not need therapists if they will just read their Bibles. He said that the Bible holds all the answers for humanity and that people need do nothing more than to read their Bibles for direction.

The lady was confused. She asked, "Are you supposed to question what I believe? Are you supposed to argue with what I've been taught for all these years? Is it right to question what you believe?" The therapist told the lady that he believed that his job was to challenge those attitudes and beliefs that disturbed his clients. If one's attitudes and beliefs are in one's best interest, then one feels good. When your beliefs cause you to shake, to lose sleep and to be very fearful, then you might conclude that your beliefs are not in your best interest. You might want to choose attitudes and beliefs that serve you better. You might want to change your beliefs to those that allow you to enjoy life and to be relatively calm and at peace with the world. If your belief in the flatness of the world keeps you from going to places you might like to visit, then you might want to give up your limiting beliefs and travel as you wish. If your belief of the devil keeps you immobilized and in the house and keeps you from enjoying life, then you might want to challenge that belief and ask yourself whether the belief makes any sense.

The human brain can believe fact or fiction. To believe that Santa Claus flies through the air with reindeer might serve you well as a child, but may *not* serve you well as an adult. You can simply question your belief in the privacy of your own room and ask yourself if it is in your best interest to continue to believe what you now hold to be true.

There are better ways to teach young people like Stinky to be well behaved than by frightening them. We do not have to lie to young people to teach them to behave properly.

This young man learned to *fear* something rather than to *value* something. He learned that he could become "bad" by making mistakes.

He learned to fear a creature that does not exist, and the negative became his focal point.

Don't lie to Stinky. Tell him about how life really is, and chances are he will make the right choices. Stinky does not want to be afraid and unhappy. Stinky wants to love and be loved. He wants to be taught the truth. He needs you to guide him. He will trust you and believe in what you tell him.

Be objective with Stinky. Tell him how things really are.

Food For Thought

- Are there adults in your life who have irrational (not in their best interest) fears such as Stinky? Please describe at least one of them.
- After reading this story, what could you tell him/her that might be helpful?
- Do you have an irrational fear comparable to Stinky? Is there something new that you could recommend to yourself, after reading this story that might help you become more peaceful?

CANDY

It was a beautiful, sunny and warm day on the west coast of Florida. The temperature was in the eighties and the humidity was low. It was simply a pleasure to be alive. It was hard to imagine there were unhappy people in the world on a day such as this. I had a peaceful morning at the office with some paperwork to complete and no students' problems to resolve.

When my lunch hour arrived, I climbed into my yellow, Jaguar XKE convertible and headed west for the short drive over the causeway to the beach along the Gulf of Mexico. The top was down on the car, the sun was warm, and the scenery could not have been more beautiful. I could smell the salt air as I drove through downtown toward the beach. The roads were crowded with tourists, both in their cars and walking, and everywhere I looked I saw people rushing off to someplace important. As I drove over the causeway to the beach I once again felt transformed into a special feeling human being. It was like closing my eyes and imagining that I was driving into paradise. There was blue-green water on both sides of the causeway, dotted with tall, green palm trees, and bushes covered with red and yellow flowers were everywhere. The scene was right out of Travel and Leisure Magazine.

Soon I was leaving the beach highway and pulling into a parking spot along the beach. I dropped some coins into a parking meter, left my shoes and socks on the floor of the E-type, hung my tie over the rearview mirror and was off across the hot sand to the water. What a wonderful feeling! The air was so very fresh, the breeze was gentle, the people on the beach were relaxing and becoming tanner by the minute, and I was at peace with the world. There seemed, for this brief period of time, to not be any significant cares in the world. All seemed at rest. Even the gulf was lapping at the shore with a gentle motion. I felt as if I had been transformed from the real world onto a new planet. It was a very peaceful experience indeed.

I recall walking along the beach for almost an hour, just enjoying the many birds in flight, the little sand crabs digging quickly out of sight as I approached, and the young and not-so-young people soaking up the warm rays of the sun. I felt renewed with energy as I walked, and I thought how I wanted everyone to have this peaceful experience.

I admit thinking that I wanted to spend the rest of my day right here on the beach, or perhaps even the rest of my life. Yet, it was time to return to the office and to respond to calls from school personnel throughout the county who had students in need of help. I had moved to Florida just six months earlier to take a position as a school psychologist.

It was a challenging and yet frustrating position for me to fill because I cared a great deal about the young people. I had the talent and skills they could utilize in resolving their personal conflicts, yet just the title of "psychologist" was enough to send parents and students alike, running away from me. I meet people even today who believe that I know what they are thinking before they utter a word. People accuse me of reading their minds. I wonder where they think I get that magical ability. I cannot read minds any better than they can.

I also meet people everyday that believe that I spent all my time analyzing others, whether they want me to or not. Even more humorous to me is the notion that I can analyze them without them speaking to me.

Some students and parents even say that I scare them because I am a psychologist. These are some of the things that I think about when I am not walking along the Gulf of Mexico, and when I get off on tangents about how to make the rest of the world happier and more content.

Anyway, it was time to turn left into the parking lot in front of my office and to focus my attention on our student population. As I entered the front door of the building, my secretary said, "Doc, you better call the principal at Eastwood High School right away! He needs your help!" I called Mr. Evans and learned that he had a student in his office that wanted to talk with me.

I left the building and walked the short distance to the high school. As I entered the principal's office, I noticed the young woman that wanted help. She was sitting next to the door, her head in her hands, with tears rolling down her cheeks.

Mr. Evans told me about Candy and her attempt to physically harm herself. She was upset about her relationship with her parents. I asked to be able to talk with Candy alone. The principal gave us his office and left. I asked Candy to tell me what was happening to her. She said something to me that I will never forget. "Dr. Brown, my parents can make me upset whenever they want to, and keep me that way for as long as they want!" She said that she was "sick of them," and wanted to "end her life." I was naturally concerned about what she said, but excited at the same time. How could I be excited about what Candy told me? I knew that her parents could not upset her, and they could not keep her upset for as long as they might choose. I knew that for a fact. They did not have that power over her. If what Candy reported was indeed factual, then you and I would simply be puppets that could be turned on and off, emotionally, by others, and we would have no self-control. This is not the case at all. We are not simply puppets under the emotional control of other people.

Now my energy would be spent teaching Candy to think factually and realistically about who she is and what she can really do. I was excited about this new relationship because I do not want young people, or any people for that matter, believing they are out of control regarding their emotional lives. I looked at Candy and told her I could help her! I said, "I know that you might not believe what I am about to tell you, but I can help you because I know that your parents do not have the power over you that you think they do, and I want to teach you how to care for yourself so you do not have to suffer as you have been." I could see by Candy's reaction she did not believe what I just told her; however, she did agree to sit still long enough to hear me out.

We have been taught beliefs that are not factual and then act as if they are. It is possible to believe that all spiders are dangerous, even though they are not. Then when one is spotted, we feel afraid though there is, in fact, nothing to fear. I believe it is important to know what and who is able to create fear in us. Is the spider the force that creates fear in us, or is fear the result of our attitudes and beliefs? It is really the fault of our attitudes and beliefs, isn't it? If we see a picture of a spider and feel fear, would we blame the picture? Ink on a sheet of paper does not have the power to cause fear in a human being. When I think scary thoughts about a spider picture, or imagine a spider crawling on me, I scare myself with the thoughts. It is my *thought* about the spider that causes the fear and not the ink, paper or image of the spider.

For the same reason, one person cannot make another person feel angry when he chooses. When I think anger-producing thoughts, then I feel anger. I control what I think, not others.

This was not easy for Candy to understand at first. Almost everything she was taught since she was born led her to believe that other people and other things cause her to feel the way she does.

Candy remembered when she was a little girl, her mother saying she had hurt her feelings by doing something her mother did not like. When Candy got her dress soiled, her mother would say, "You make Mommy feel bad when you get your dress dirty!" Candy might stop to visit with a friend on the way home from school and arrive home later than expected. Her mother would say, "You worried me when you did not come home from school on time!"

I think her mother meant well. She taught her daughter what she believed to be true. Her mother believed that Candy was the cause of her hurt feelings, and the cause of her worry, and she told her so.

The fact is that Candy's soiled dress cannot, and did not cause her mother's upset feelings. It was not the soiled dress, nor Candy, that was responsible for the mother's discomfort. Her mother may have believed that her little girl should do as she asked, and when Candy soiled her dress her mother was disappointed. She did not get the results she wanted. Her mother expected her daughter's dress to remain clean. When she got a typical little girl with a soiled dress, she was disappointed and perhaps even angry. She didn't get what she wanted. The belief that her little girl should absolutely not get dirt on her dress was the upsetting factor, not the dirty dress. Candy didn't know that. She loved and believed her mother. If her mother said she got her dress dirty, and hurt her mother's feelings, then most likely she did. Candy was learning to believe that she could hurt her mother's feelings even though it was not possible to do so.

When Candy forgot to be a responsible little girl and did not arrive home on time, her mother would worry. Her mother likely learned that "a good mother worries about her children," and, "children are a worry to their parents," and even, "if a mother worries about her children it will help." Well, it is possible for Candy to come home late from school and her mother not to have worried about her. Mom has an alternative to worry. What is it? Her mother might have remembered that she gave Candy permission to stop for a visit with her girlfriend on her way home. Her mother could walk to her friends to look for her, or make some phone calls. Her mother could call the school to see if someone had seen Candy after school. Her mother could remember that Candy found her way home lots of times previous to this, and is likely to come home safely tonight.

When life does not go as we plan or expect, we tend to imagine the worst happening, and it almost never does.

Anyway, Candy learned that she controlled the way her mother felt. She learned that she could drive her teachers up the wall if she wanted. She learned that she could give her dad a headache when he came home from work. She learned that she could drive her sister crazy. She had lots of emotional power at a very young age. The problem was Candy believed her parents had the same power over her. They can make her angry whenever they want, and keep her that way for as long as they choose. This is make-believe-power that only seems to be real!

Candy, because of her early childhood education, was willing to believe that her parents had this ability. So, when her parents gave her a reason to make herself angry, she did as they expected. When they did what was required for Candy to be upset for days, Candy kept herself upset for days. The beliefs that Candy was using to upset herself were old and well learned. The excitement was that Candy could change! She could learn new responses to old parental behaviors.

Candy controls what she thinks, not her parents. Candy's attitudes and beliefs control her emotions, not her parents'. Candy is in charge of Candy. She just doesn't know it yet.

Imagine believing that you are in prison and cannot escape, but the next day finding the key to your cell in your own pocket. The path to freedom is free for the taking. That is what Candy was about to find out.

If you ever believed that someone else controlled your emotional life when you would rather they didn't have the power, then you also have something to gain from what Candy was about to learn. It is fun for me to find someone who seems emotionally hopeless and to demonstrate they indeed have the ability to climb out of the hopelessness. Finding solutions to problems where we see only hopelessness is thrilling. Once we see we have the ability to erase hopelessness under one set of circumstances, we find it easier to see the light at the end of the tunnel next time.

The poem, "I Am Your Master," explains, "Our Master" is our own attitudes and beliefs, not something external to us. Our thoughts can make us happy and they can make us sad. They can be the love we share, or create the hatred by which we hurt others. My thoughts are the vehicles used on the Florida beach to transport myself to paradise. There are others complaining on the very same beach that it is too hot, there is nothing to do, or wishing they were some place nicer.

Candy was a willing subject because she felt lousy. She felt that way for a long time. She could not see a healthy way out of the misery, only that of harming herself. I wanted to offer her an alternative! Is it possible that a significant portion of our suffering is self-imposed?

We don't suffer like this because we want to, or because we are sick. We upset ourselves the way we do because we have had good, if not great, role models. Television Soap Operas are popular teachers of how others create our sadness, anger, hatred and fears. Our best and favorite teachers taught us that we controlled their emotional lives, and they controlled ours.

There is little good to come from blaming them. Other people only teach us to think and believe as they do. We cannot expect more from them. If they had known better they would have been different role models. They were the role models they knew how to be.

One day Candy came home late from school. She was not doing anything that she ought to be ashamed of, but she was indeed late to help her mother with the dinner chores. By the time Candy arrived home, her mother was angry. When Candy entered the kitchen door, her mother unloaded her anger on her. In the process of yelling at Candy for this lateness and others, she said, "You are nothing but a whore!" Those were strong words to hear with strong meanings attached. Candy rushed to her room and slammed the door. She did not come out for supper, and stayed in her room until it was time to come out for school the next day.

When Candy saw me at school the next day she told me what her mother had done. She told me how she went to her room and did not come out that evening. She said that it was her mother's fault and it was her mother who ruined the evening.

I had to agree that if Candy's mother called her a whore, it would not be fun and might be a shock. I could not agree that it was her mother who "hurt her feelings" and "spoiled the evening." In fact, when I asked Candy's mother to come in to talk with me, she said that she never for a moment thought that her daughter was a whore, or that she ought to spend any time in her room for what she had done. She said she wanted her daughter to be home on time to help her prepare dinner. Her mother had a very busy day at her job and really wanted her daughter's help. When her mother did not get what she wanted that afternoon, she made herself especially angry with all her thoughts about what she wanted and didn't get. She wanted her daughter to do what she wanted her to do! By the time Candy arrived home, her mother was saying things she did not mean. Her mom had plenty of time to upset herself waiting for her daughter.

What happened had happened, and I wanted Candy to know that she also had a <u>choice</u> about how to behave. She could have asked her mother how she could help at the late hour. She could have offered to wash the dishes after dinner to make up for her lateness. Candy knew she was not a whore, so why send herself to her room for something she was not.

We've all learned such intense emotional reactions to some words and phrases. If Candy's mother called her a "tennis shoe," she would most likely have laughed. Candy never learned to be angry when called a tennis shoe. She surely learned to upset herself when called a whore! Who upsets whom? Do you see my point? Do you understand you really do have an alternative? Do you understand you do have control over what you feel, emotionally? I wanted Candy to understand. I wanted her to understand her mother was angry. It is easy for us to take ownership of someone else's upset, and make ourselves upset at the same time. We, however, have a <u>choice</u>. We don't have to be angry just because someone else invites us. Does that sound strange? Does it sound strange to hear that when Candy walked into the house and her mother invited her to be angry, she had <u>choices</u>? Candy was angry long after her mother calmed down and relaxed in front of the television for the evening.

Candy's mother invited her daughter to join her in her angry mood. She gave her a good reason with her choice of words, and she used a higher volume voice to send her the message. Most of us have <u>learned</u> to feel insulted in that particular situation. Candy was no exception.

Candy's mom set the stage for Candy's potential academy award performance. When Candy saw the stage all prepared for her, she hopped right on it and did her best to receive a nomination. What if Lady Gaga gave an outstanding performance one evening in concert and then blamed her parents for making her do it? Who was indeed performing? Who was singing? Who was making who do what? I believe that you are getting the message.

Close your eyes for a moment. Imagine one of the worst things that ever happened to you in your life. Imagine it being as awful as it was. Imagine the original people in the scene. Imagine them saying what they did. See yourself in the picture. Feel the way you felt when the situation was actually taking place. Imagine that nothing changed. Notice that you cannot change them still. What is the <u>one thing</u> that you can change? Allow the other people to do what they did. Allow them to say what they said. What is the one thing <u>you</u> can change to help you feel better almost instantly?

If you change the way you think about the people, what they are doing and saying, then you will come away from the memory feeling significantly different. Its not actually what they said or did that caused your upset, rather how you evaluated their behavior.

Sometimes we don't like what we see or hear from others. We prefer they talk or act differently. But, they talk, or behave, as <u>they</u> prefer, instead. Consider a past situation. Make yourself think differently about what happened to you. Make yourself look differently at the situation. If you thought he stabbed you in the back, take another look at the situation. Did you get stabbed in the back, or did he do something the way he wanted, and not as you wanted? It makes a difference.

What's the difference? What's the difference what Candy thinks? The difference is almost everything! If she thinks her mother stabbed her in the back for being late, she feels rotten. If she remembered that she promised to be home right after school to help her mother prepare dinner for her friends and family, and she was late, she might decide to apologize and get busy helping her. The benefit of thinking differently is that we feel less miserable. We recognize that our emotional reactions are indeed ours. We take responsibility for them. We own our own reactions. We utilize our choices, one being feeling less miserable.

<u>When we think for ourselves, and don't just react through habit, we have increased personal power over anger, hate, fear, sadness, depression, contentment and happiness. Those are enough reasons to change some of our attitudes and beliefs. I have never enjoyed feeling badly, have you?</u>

Candy was a high school student who had suffered significantly in the last several years. She didn't want to, but she believed that others were responsible for her unhappiness. She believed she had to get what she wanted from others. She believed others had to behave, as she wanted. I told her that she had the right and ability to upset herself whenever she didn't get what she wanted. She also had the right to change her thinking about her life.

She didn't like being called names by her mother. She loves her mother and she wants her mother to love her. She wants her mother to respect her. Sometimes her mother is tired, hungry, or frustrated with life. Sometimes her mother does not behave like Candy prefers. But, it is only a preference of Candy's. Candy does not have to get what she wants to be relatively calm. Candy is experienced enough to recognize anger in her mother and not demand that her mother treat her gently and kindly at that moment. Candy admitted that. When Candy wants one mood from her mother, and gets yet another, Candy can chose to walk softly and wait till her mother's mood changes. Candy could even offer her mother a sincere apology for her lateness, along with a hug and a smile.

I might refuse to give a Popsicle to a child when asked, but I am not responsible for the tears that follow. I may have to stop for a red light when I am late for a meeting, but I can choose how to think, and therefore feel, while waiting for the light to change. I have some significant choices. I have lots of choices!

Candy was listening to me, but she appeared not to believe. She accused me of being some kind of machine that never felt anything. She suggested that perhaps I never felt anything. I told her that I could get angry if I wanted to, and sometimes I did out of old habit. I have feelings like others. I just don't want her to go to her room angry and spend the night there if she would rather be somewhere else. It might be nice if next time she were in her room feeling upset, she could insightfully remember that she did not "have to" be there. She could remind herself to redefine how she got there, and who is responsible for her being there. She might just end her suffering earlier than before. That would be an improvement! Often, it's simply a matter of degree, rather than feeling "perfectly" happy or "perfectly" upset. Practice leads to improvement.

Candy said she hopes each time her mother gets upset it will never happen again. The next time her mother is upset, Candy acts surprised and suffers all over again. Yes, Candy's mother could change. But, Candy is more in a position to change herself than change her mother. She will be more successful changing herself.

Candy could have more realistic expectations about her mother, and feel less threatened at the same time. Candy can expect that when she does not do what her mother asks, her mother will respond with anger toward her. If Candy realized the connection, then she would not be so "surprised and shocked" when encountering her mother's anger. "When I don't do what I promised to do, my mother is going to react in an angry fashion," she could say to herself. "I promised to be home on time tonight and I am late. My mother is going to be upset with me when I enter the house!"

Candy could also remember that Dr. Brown said, "Your mother is not responsible for how <u>you</u> feel. <u>You</u> are! Make an effort to comply with your mother's wishes and save yourself the hassle. That way you can <u>add</u> to the harmony in your family. In this case, <u>you</u> were in error in the first place. You didn't keep <u>your</u> promise and then acted surprised when your mother was upset. You could have predicted her reaction. If you THINK about it, YOU KNOW BETTER,

Reeducation does not come without practice. Our early education did not come without practice, sweat and lots of tears. The new education is not going to come without practice, sweat and perhaps some tears either. But, <u>it is possible to change</u>, that's the good news!

I am able to watch television wherein people are upset, crying, sad, or angry. I don't feel the way they do. I can watch others be upset and not feel the same. It is possible to see others upset and not experience their feelings myself. It is possible for Candy's mother to be upset, and Candy to remain calm. It <u>is</u> possible!

The most important person in this situation is Candy. She is asking for help. She wants to hurt less. She wants to understand herself better. Candy needs to know what her options are, and how to feel better without the use of drugs and other chemicals.

Candy has emotional alternatives, if and when she wants to practice them. She has been told that her emotions are <u>learned</u> reactions. Reeducation is possible for her. She knows the change requires practice. The new education will take as long as it takes, depending on her motivation to change. Each of us has varying motivational levels with varying intensities. Sometimes, the more we are hurting, the more we are motivated to change. That was certainly a factor in Candy's case.

She was learning to imagine a past situation and imagine how to think and behave differently in her mind. This is a safe and effective way in which to practice feeling and behaving differently next time a similar situation occurs. Imagination is a powerful tool in the reeducation process.

Candy seemed to understand that an invitation to argue did not have to be honored. She had the potential to learn to remain relatively calm when others around her are upset. The upset of others does not necessitate her being upset. Candy was learning that a fellow human being can't make her feel the way she chooses not to feel. Her mother cannot make her happy or sad, not really! We are not emotional puppets. We have lots of choices and alternatives, even when we think we do not.

I told Candy that when she gets to the point of thinking that she has run out of options, to remember what Dr. Brown says, "You do have choices. You are not aware of them at the moment, but you have some! If you can't think of them, ask me."

Please read the Little Golden Book, The Little Engine That Could. In fact, read it twice. The message is an important one for all of us. The big engine could not pull the cars over the hill because he thought, "They are too heavy a load." The Little Engine came along and pulled the cars over the mountain while chugging the thought, "I think I can ... I think I can ... I think I can." Those thoughts won't make all things possible, but they sure will free us to do more than we are presently doing. We will also feel less hopeless. Try it right now, "I think I can, I think I can, and really do think I can!"

What we think makes all the difference. Our thinking is our master. It can make us weak, or strong. It can make us happy or sad. It can allow us to try, or it can build a wall around us so we go nowhere. Thinking can reeducate us to be more the kind of person we want to be, or it can keep us down on ourselves and angry. It can make us love, or it can make us hate. It can create options and alternatives, or it can keep us in our bedrooms angry with others.

Candy was learning to think thoughts of herself and her mother that are more in her own best interest. She understands that <u>Candy</u> is responsible for <u>Candy's behavior</u>, not her mother.

I wish that I could introduce you to Candy today. She is a changed person. She suffers much less because she has taken responsibility for her own behavior. She has taken back the control that she once believed she had lost. The relationship between Candy and her mother has changed. Candy has been able to share what she is learning with her mother. That has been of benefit to both women.

Candy practices her newfound education daily, and I expect she'll only get better and better with time …

Food For Thought

- Who in your life has seemingly been able to upset you and keep you that way for longer than you wanted?
- What did he or she do to upset you?
- What specifically can you do today to become more in charge of your own emotional life?
- What do you have to think differently about yourself?
- What do you have to think differently about other people?

ANALYSIS OF ATTITUDES

"My ex-husband was the one who upset my world. He cheated on me with other women. When I found out I thought it was the end of my life! I immediately asked myself, "What did I do wrong?" I believed that I could not let anyone else know my marriage had failed. What would they think of me? After a year of soul-searching I realized it was <u>not</u> my fault and there ought to be life-after-divorce for me. I loved myself enough to know that I was not the problem here, he was. It was time for me to cut my losses and move on to a better life. Today, life is good!"

I think that if your husband cheats on you with other women, it ought to be the end of <u>his</u> life, not yours. Yes? He is in error, not you.

It does seem "normal" for the spouse of the cheater to look at herself as having done something wrong to "make" the cheating husband cheat. My goodness, we are so willing to accept responsibility for someone else's behavior! Imagine, "I forced him to break our wedding vows and sneak around the city having sex with other women! I am not sure <u>how</u> I did it, but I must have done it or he would be happy and sleeping only with me. There is nothing wrong with him that could have caused this abnormal behavior. It must be me!" We must have been watching too many Soap Operas.

It took a YEAR for you to realize that it is HE who is in the wrong!? Yes, there is life-after-divorce and YOU are the one who deserves it! You finally realized, after a year of introspection and suffering, that it was TIME to give yourself a better, more enjoyable life. Wonderful news! Yes indeed, it is time to start treating yourself as the beautiful, worthwhile human being that you are.

And, one more thing, your marriage did not "fail." Your husband <u>destroyed</u> it! One person cannot make a marriage, but one person can indeed destroy it, and that's what he did. He did it. It is his fault.

Today, your life is good. Congratulations!

Doc

— — —

"My mother is the only one who could make me upset and keeps me that way. She told me many times that she has had a terrible life and most of the things I do keep her that way. My sister says our mother has been depressed for as long as she can remember and my sister is 58. I have always felt badly for my mother, but I am realizing that no matter what I do, or could have done, my mother would not change. I have decided to only take responsibility for <u>my</u> feelings and stop being responsible for my mom's. I am going to set an example for my son."

Your personal decision to take better care of yourself is exciting to read. Congratulations to you! Many children attempt to take responsibility for their parents' emotional lives instead of their own, and fail miserably. It isn't because the children don't work at it night and day. It is because the children CANNOT be responsible for anyone's emotional life, other than their own. It's just that simple.

Your mother is responsible for her own thoughts and feelings, not you. You are responsible for your thoughts and feelings. You cannot adopt your mother's emotional life and run it for her. That's HER job. She can attempt to blame you for doing a lousy job herself, but her case would never hold up in court! She is to blame for her lousy life, NOT you. That's such GOOD news for you! Rejoice in this good news. Love yourself. Treat yourself to some newfound freedom from blame. You didn't make your mother's life miserable; she did! That may well be too bad, but it is NOT your fault.

You be responsible for your emotional life. Do a better job with yours than your mother has done with hers. Enjoy!

I wish you happiness.

Doc

– – –

"My mother nags & nags me. I try not to listen. She always finds something to fight about. I could do what she asks so I would not have to hear the nagging. I could be more understanding & cooperative. I could do what she says."

Let's see. You blame your mom for nagging at you. You wish she'd STOP that! The effort you make is "not to listen to her." In the next breath you seem to clearly outline the solutions to your problem. "If I did as she asked…if I was more understanding and cooperative…and if I followed her rules (while living in HER house) then…she would not nag at me."

So WHY complain about a situation it appears YOU have control over? Give your mother what she wants while in her home and the nagging will stop. Or, move out, get a job, get a place of your own, and do as you please…

For your self-report, it appears that the problem is NOT your mother and her nagging. The problem is _____. You guessed it!

Good luck with this,

Doc

— — —

"Just recently (1 year, 4 months) I began dating my current girlfriend. Our time together has been, and will continue to be, a pleasure. She knows how to push my buttons! Sometimes my aggravation with her is so bad my eye twitches with disgust. She is stubborn. She considers herself right 85% of the time. I transformed her from being the ugliest (attitude and personality-wise) person to a rose ready to blossom, but the road to this point was extremely bumpy.

Often I find myself in a men's shoe store looking for a new pair of shoes to wear. When I spot something that "looks good," I tend to ask the salesperson to let me try a pair on. It is in trying them on that I find a reason to buy them or reasons to leave them in the store. The "looking good" needs to be tested by wearing them for a moment or two; getting better acquainted with them, if you will.

If they don't fit, I never buy them with the intention of wearing them till they do, or taking them home to modify, and then wear. I really do make every effort, if I find them initially appealing, to see if they are wearable. Do they fit? Are they initially comfortable? Do they enhance my outfit? Could we grow to be friends?

I don't spend any time whatsoever, attempting to force them to be something they are not.

But you, on the other hand are in the business of reconstruction. Perhaps you ought to open a "Re-Construction Company for Aggravating Women." You sound like you know your business.

On the other hand, I wonder if it wouldn't be easier and more fun to "shop" a bit longer and find a woman who is closer to your needs and expectations from the beginning. It sounds like both you and she had a rough year and a half together. I wonder what <u>she</u> thinks of the reconstruction process she went through under your supervision.

Today she is a "rose ready to blossom." Does this mean she is not yet the woman you are comfortable being with? She needs more of your expertise and reconstruction? I am concerned for you both! Now that you are almost complete with <u>your</u> rebuilding, does she need or want to do the same with you? Perhaps if you made her into what <u>you</u> really want, it also means that you have convinced her that <u>you</u> require no modifications.

It would be interesting to me, to hear <u>her</u> side of the story.

I am not convinced. You started your notes to me saying, "Our time together has been, and will continue to be, a pleasure."

Many people, much smarter than I, have written, "Friendship is the most important ingredient in a lasting relationship." I do hope that somewhere in your dating process, you find a friend, even a best friend, who needs little or no reconstruction. That's my wish for you both …

Peace,

Doc

– – –

"My daughter seemingly has the power to upset me at will and keep me that way. I think I am usually the cause. I get angry at her for being a smart ass, for being rude, for not doing her chores, etc. Then when I yell and tell her how upset SHE has made me, if she doesn't get upset I continue to yell and cry until she is feeling the same as I am. That's not fair to her. It's not fair to me either. I notice I do the same thing with my boyfriend when he does not treat me the way I think he should. I also give him the silent treatment until I see that he feels bad for hurting my feelings. I will then be happy when I see that he feels badly. How crazy it that? I know I need to think differently but I'm not sure what I should be thinking. I don't know how to handle disappointment. I expect my children to behave as I want them to, and I expect my boyfriend to respect me."

First of all, your daughter does NOT have power over your emotional life. YOU do! YOU decide WHEN to be upset. YOU decide WHAT to upset yourself about. YOU decide how to LOOK and how to ACT while you are upset. And, YOU decide HOW LONG to keep yourself upset. You LEARNED the emotional habits that you have today. YOU can UNLEARN the habits that you don't prefer to keep and you can LEARN new reactions to your daughter and to others. YOU are IN CONTROL of your emotional life, whether you believe it or not. YOU are in the emotional driver's seat, each and everyday, in your life. Think about this, seriously.

Secondly, it is reasonable for you to want your daughter to treat you with love and respect. It is also reasonable for you to want your daughter to help with the household chores. However, history would tell us that children are not in the habit of volunteering to help around the house. They need training and persistence from us to learn that habit. That training can be fraught with inconvenience and frustration on the part of parents. However, the amount of anger, rage, screaming, pouting and crying on the part of the parents is the decision and choice of the parents, not the children. It is inconvenient to have our children resist our attempts to educate them, but it just might be the norm. Therefore, as long as it is already inconvenient to have to teach them, it is even more damn inconvenient to upset ourselves too. It is as though we have not suffered enough with time and time again having to tell our kids to clean their rooms; we additionally choose to make ourselves feel rotten in the process.

As a professor, I can tell my students, over and over again, how I want them to do their assignments. They choose to do it as they prefer. I have chosen to not upset myself when they do as they please and simply continue to repeat my preferences again and again until they get it right. Some never do as I want. Some children seldom do as their parents' request.

I heard a wonderful phrase, years ago, from one of my favorite professors. He said, "I suggest you refuse to upset yourself without damn good reason." Often I say to myself, "I refuse to upset myself without damn good reason, and you are not a damn good reason!" Then I chuckle to myself and move on with my day. You could choose to do the same with your daughter, or anyone else you choose.

This business of "lack of fairness" that you talk about is right on! Your upset with your daughter has little value. You get upset, the she gets upset, and you both share your upsets with each other. Nothing is accomplished. You could choose to talk to her. Tell her what you expect, calmly, and ask what would be needed to have her comply with your wishes. One friend of mine became so exasperated with her daughter that she let her live in the "filth" of her own room. Eventually she graduated from high school and moved out. I don't recommend it, but it might be better than your continuous upset with your daughter. You deserve a more peaceful life, with or without having a daughter with a clean room. I am interested in "options" and "alternatives" in living that allow me to experience a more peaceful lifestyle. You said you are confused about "what to think," so I am making some suggestions for you to consider.

I expect my children to do as I want sometimes, not all the time. If I expect them to do what I want all the time, I am disappointed more often. I don't like to be disappointed, so I do my best to keep my expectations in line with what I can really expect them to do as chilcren. I rejoice when they do as I expect. When they do as they please, I make an effort to understand their reasoning. Often their reasoning makes sense to me. Sometimes their reasoning makes more sense than mine. Ha!

And, you want your boyfriend to respect you. That means to me that you have some preconceived notions as to how you want to be treated. Have you made sincere efforts to clearly define how you want him to treat you? If not, that might help you both. I believe that my wife loves me dearly, but sometimes she treats me in ways I don't immediately understand. I wonder why she is treating me in such a manner and I do my best to get her to explain her behavior. Most often her explanations clear up my confusion. Sometimes, however, I just accept the behavior as something I don't understand, and don't have to understand, and I move on. I don't want to upset myself without damn good reason, and this event in my life is not a damn good reason! See how that works? Try it, you might really like it.

Love yourself a little more. Look in the mirror and decide that you like you. Other people's love and approval is not necessary at this very moment for you to be acceptable and loveable to yourself. Look at your image in the mirror and smile. Just feel good looking at yourself in the mirror. Imagine something positive in the reflection. You are worthy of good feelings. Enjoy your moment. Then, move on...

Now I feel better, having written to you. Thanks...

Doc

– – –

"My boyfriend comes home at 6:30 in the morning or after 2 days of being gone. I have two choices, the way I see it. I can decide that I don't want this kind of life and get out of the relationship, or I can learn not to get upset about his behavior."

I would spend NO time learning to put up with his behavior. You can find a man on any street corner in town to treat you that way. I would leave the relationship immediately and find a real boyfriend, one who loves you and respects you! Really, I would!

Doc

– – –

"The mother of my daughter gets me so upset. Her attitude always drives my crazy. She somehow feels I owe her something. It makes me crazy."

It is difficult for me to understand your situation because of the limited information you have shared with me. But, I would say, "You OWE the mother of your daughter more than something! You were a partner in bringing your daughter into this world and you owe 'the mother of your daughter' at least some significant financial support." A man is someone who helps make a baby AND stays around to raise AND love the baby until she can care for herself.

I'd say the mother of your daughter has a point and YOU ought to LISTEN to what SHE has to say. If you do not, I hope the law catches up with you very soon.

Doc

— — —

"My brother-in-law has lived with us for the past 5-1/2 years. He has a habit of using the bathroom in the mornings without closing the door. I need to realize that even though we have discussed this with him several times, he is not going to change his routine. I will choose to ignore the situation and not allow it to upset me any longer."

You are certainly free to ignore his lack of cooperation with you. However, I do have something additional for you to consider.

I have been a student of "Tough Love" for many years. We have rules in our house and we have expected our children to follow them. We also have clear rules (expectations) for friends and family when they visit in our home. Your brother-in-law is a guest in your home. You want him to close the bathroom door when he uses the bathroom. He won't comply with your wishes even though you have been generous enough to give him shelter. He then has two choices; (1) Close the bathroom door as requested, or (2) Get out of your home immediately.

Makes sense to me. How about you?

Doc

— — —

"My father left before I was born. I have 2 older brothers that were about 3 and 4 when he left. My father would call 2 weeks after my birthday and tell me he was sorry to be calling me so late, but he was coming to visit me. He would never show up. Every time I heard his voice on the phone I cried on the inside. This continued to happen until I was sixteen. No Merry Christmas…no congratulations when I graduated from high school…and no more late happy birthdays. He just stopped communicating with me. I now know that only I can

make me happy! I don't depend on anyone to put a smile on my face. I'm making me happy now by going to school. I think I'm a much stronger and wiser person. I believe that people set their own moods. We decide what we want and whom we want it with. As you say, Dr. Brown, "Life is good!"

I am proud of you and your new-found insights. Thank you for sharing your thoughts with me!

Doc

— — —

"People say things just to hurt my feelings."

I am sure you are correct. People play all kinds of silly and hurtful games. Some people are especially adept at being rude, uncaring and mean. There are plenty of reasons in a day to feel badly. But, YOU have CHOICES about how to react to people's comments and actions.

On occasion, someone gives me the "finger." When I see that symbol in the air, I recognize it as an INVITATION. It is an "invitation for upset." It says, "I am miserable and I invite you to join me in my misery." Because I see it as an invitation to make myself upset along with the other person, I have choices. There was a time in my life when I might well have joined him in his misery. Today I haven't the time or the interest. I simply recognize the other person as hurting and even, on occasion, have some empathy for the poor man. Often I smile inside and say to myself, "Another time perhaps. I have better things to expend my energy on at the moment. Do call again." Ha!

The good news is that we have CHOICES about how to act when other people invite us to join their upset.

Gary Walker was my Jujitsu instructor. He taught me that when confronted with some aggression, the first and best response is to BACK UP a few steps. This tends to reduce some of the aggressor's forward momentum and gives me a few more moments to decide what MY next move will be. There is another good suggestion. Just because the other person is asking, or demanding, that I respond to them, I don't have to respond that instant. I can take a few steps back and THINK about what the best CHOICE is for me to make.

People talk and people say most anything. Regardless of what is said, I decide what my reaction will be. Most of what I hear is not worth a serious reaction on my part. Certainly most of what I hear is NOT worth upsetting me about.

I wish you peace,

Doc

— — —

"My sister-in-law has got me so upset that I don't even like to be around her anymore. We used to go out to eat with her and my brother-in-law but she always makes fun of everyone and controls the whole conversation. Her husband won't even speak during dinner because she always makes fun of him. I have decided not to torture myself anymore and not hang around with her. I don't need the abuse. I am a good person and she can make fun of all the people she wants but I won't be a part of it."

Unfortunately, we don't get to choose our relatives. Some of them can indeed be no fun to be around. You have the perfect right to CHOOSE who you will have dinner with, and who will not be sitting at your table. That seems to make more sense than allowing someone to ruin your meal. I smile when I hear of someone who is exercising their right to make their world a happier place in which to live. It would appear you made a wise, personal decision.

Thanks for sharing,

Doc

— — —

"My boyfriend makes comments that I find hurtful. He carefully watches the things I do. He will physically reject me sexually for a number of days and then turn to porn. He will leave traces of what he has done to try to upset me."

I really hope you don't need me to give you this advice. I hope you have already made the decision to FIND A NEW BOYFRIEND. Get out of this relationship and find someone who is FIRST your friend and secondly, someone who RESPECTS you. Accept NOTHING less. YOU DESERVE BETTER!!!

Doc

\- \- \-

"I get very frustrated with my daughter. Up until reading <u>Candy</u> I thought my frustration was all her fault. I have certain expectations in mind as to how children are supposed to behave and when they do not behave as I expect I get very frustrated and upset with them. The truth is, there is no 'certain way' children should act. All children have differing personalities and they all behave differently. Maybe I should look at the characteristics of my daughter's personality and factor that into my 'certain way she should behave' philosophy. That will help me to have more patience and not get so uptight with her."

You make a great deal of sense. Children's personalities do vary and it is important to pay attention to their differences. Children require lots of education and training from their parents. There is nothing wrong with having rules and expectations for them to follow. However, they don't follow ALL the rules any better than adults do. Learning to RAISE your FRUSTRATION TOLERANCE LEVEL and still be a quality parent and teacher is worth the time and effort involved on both your parts.

I'm proud that you were able to read this story, make sense of it AND apply some of the ideas to your personal life. It appears that you and I did NOT come out of our mothers with an "Instruction Manual" and therefore we have lots to learn about our lives and our relationships with others. Education can be a VERY REWARDING process indeed.

I wish you lots of quality education and success with your daughter.

Peace,

Doc

– – –

"Right now my life is one big emotional mess and being more in charge of it is impossible at this day and time!"

NOT "impossible." Little if anything is impossible. You are a POWERFUL woman and almost nothing is "impossible" for you. Geeeeezzzzzz! If nothing else, take a walk around the block, or on a nearby beach. Whistle a happy tune as you walk. Look up at the blue sky and be thankful you are alive to enjoy this moment. FAKE IT! Pretend this day is YOURS and LIFE IS GOOD. Tell yourself whatever cheers you. Remember a good time that you have had. Stick your chest out, and lift your chin up. Force a smile on your face. ACT in charge of YOUR life and feel GOOD for a moment. One moment of peace and calm is better than nothing. Once you have that first moment mastered, the second will be a piece of cake.

You are in college classes 8 to 12 hours a week. That can be and is a respite for you. Your professor is on your side. Education is the game being played. It is growthful and not harmful. The room is air conditioned and the humidity is low. Your classmates are non-aggressive and friendly. There are calm, peaceful peers for you to chat with. Life is good, for the moment. Rejoice in the moment! Think about the **positive** aspects of the moment. You are safe ... growing educationally ... in a comfortable environment ... achieving an important personal goal ... with people who genuinely care about you ... and the "emotional mess" that was perhaps part of your day is no longer with you.

YOU are IN CHARGE now! Smile as you count the **positive** aspects of your evening.

Do as I have suggested. Gain some additional self-control and more self-respect. Your world is NOT in charge of your emotional life, YOU are!

Enjoy something, everyday. YOU are WORTH it!
Doc

– – –

"I was raised having only one parent. My father was not around. He left my mother to be with another woman and started another family with her. When I was 17 years old I decided to move in with my father and start my life somewhere new. He said he would help me with whatever I needed. He made lots of promises to me but he never kept them. He had a daughter with his other wife. He treated her much better than he treated me. When it comes right down to it, my father has been the source of my upset for most of my life. I work a fulltime job and am attending college fulltime. I'm the only one in the family that has graduated from high school and the only one to go to college. Yet he treats me as though I am a bad child. My father recently told me I had to move out of his house but my half-sister could stay. It's hard! I understand that I am 20 years old but I am not presently in a position to move out. My sister is a high school dropout and has a child. She has no job and my father does everything for her. I just don't think it's fair! I just wish I could know why he wants to make me feel like I am not good enough. As of today, I am going to take better care of me! I am no longer going to care what he thinks about me and I don't care if I'm not good enough for him. I know I am good enough for me. I have accomplished a great deal. I think that as long as I have faith in myself I don't need anyone's support. I thought that I needed my father. I thought I needed him to tell me he is proud of me, but I never heard that from him. Treating me the way he has only makes me hold a grudge against him. But, I know I have to change that. I know that holding grudges is not worth it. I can change my attitude and put the past behind me. I will strive for my future and know that no one is going to hold me back! I am my own supporter!! (-:

First of all, I am PROUD of YOU! And, let me say without reservation, YOU are GOOD enough!! In fact, you are doing an outstanding job with your life!!! You have all the excuses you need to act out, and instead, you are making POSITIVE choices and taking POSITIVE actions with your life. YOU are to be CONGRATULATED!!!

Men and women need only the proper "plumbing" to be parents. They don't need any skills. They aren't required to know how-to parent. They aren't required to understand loving relationships. They only have to be like any other animal to reproduce. Some parents are no better than snakes that crawl on their bellies on the ground! Men aren't men because they can "make" a baby. Men are men because they know how-to raise a baby. Your "father" isn't a man. He is simply a member of the male gender, and sadly so.

Ok, enough of that. The important point here is that YOU are doing a fine job with yourself, and you are very correct when you say, "No one is going to hold me back. I am my own supporter!!"

I believe YOU know how to proceed with your life. I believe YOU are on the right track. I believe YOU will continue to be SUCCESSFUL. If you need help along the way, call me collect.

Once again, **I am very proud of you!**

Doc

– – –

THE DEATH CALL

My first presentation of an introduction to Rational Thinking for senior high school psychology students went well. The majority of the students seemed to be listening and taking notes about what was being said. However, in the middle of the second class, I was accused of telling the students that they should not have <u>any</u> emotions. One girl in particular, accused me of sounding like a computer that acts and behaves without emotion, a machine that has no fun. At this point, I explained that what I was excited about was <u>controlling</u> my emotional life so that I suffered less, and was calm and even happier more often. I was not saying that we could do away with our emotions altogether. I told the students that I could get angry, or not get angry, as I choose. Since <u>my</u> brain controls <u>my</u> emotions, I have the ability to not be angry and upset if I choose not to be. I can learn emotional control just as I learn physical control.

The same girl spoke again. "OK," she said. "Let's suppose that everything is the same now in this room with the exception that we add a phone on your desk. The phone rings, you answer it, and a voice on the other end that you recognize and trust tells you that your wife has just died. My question, Dr. Brown, is <u>now</u> how are you going to feel? Your wife has just died and here you are telling us how great Rational Thinking and this new learning about emotions can be. What are <u>you</u> going to feel now?"

I must admit that this question was not included in the "teacher's guide." I hesitated a moment and then told class, "You are expecting me to say something special. Would you please tell me how you believe I <u>should</u> feel and how long I <u>should</u> feel that way?" The 34 students, without exception, thought I should feel bad, sad and/or unhappy for a period of time ranging from nine months to one year. The student who initially asked the question said, "All right, you know what we expect. So tell us how you would feel when you answered the phone!"

In reply I asked the class what their response would be if they noticed, after a moment or so, that I had a gentle smile on my face. Someone said, "You would have to have not loved your wife!" "You would be some kind of animal," said another. "You would not be human," came a third response. I then asked them to recall one of the most important ideas that I had shared with them a week before: "We feel the way we do because of the thoughts we think. We can control what thoughts we want to think, and therefore feel the way we want to feel." I told the class of some beautiful moments regarding our wedding day, of some wonderful trips to the mountains and streams or southeast Arizona, of the birth of our child that we delivered together, of our first home in Florida and of some personally wonderful times we recently had together.

The class apparently forgot themselves for a moment, because the girl who had asked the death-feeling question now said, "Gee, those times sound very special to you and make me feel warm inside." At that moment a very important insight took place. Now the students could understand the soft smile on my face at a moment when they expected sorrow and pain. How could thoughts of beautiful moments with someone I love produce sadness? It was true I had the choice at the moment to think thoughts like, "She is gone and I will never see her again," or "I certainly am going to miss her." Those thoughts would surely lead to feelings of sadness. The choice, however, of which thoughts and feelings to have, is up to me.

I then insisted that the class hear one other admission. I told them I was not perfect, that I would die a fallible human being just as I was born, and therefore I would never completely master the use of Rational Thinking. While I could not be sure how I would react if and when I receive that "phone call," I could tell them now that through a practiced understanding of Rational Thinking I would be sad and depressed only as long as I decided to make myself sad and depressed.

That was not the last class period I spent with those students however. Some of them still meet with me individually on my visits to their school to share with me their work in rational emotional re-education. As an end to this personally exciting experience, I received a call from the mother of the girl that asked me to respond to the "death call." The mother reported, "Something wonderful had happened to the relationship between her and her daughter." "The two of us have fought for the past seventeen years and we have not had a very happy relationship. A couple of months ago my daughter came home, looked at me and said that she was never again going to make herself angry at me. You know, Dr. Brown, we have had a wonderful new relationship because she refuses to get angry with me and therefore I have a hard time staying angry with her. We really work out the problems together somehow now. I sure hope that you continue to do to my daughter whatever you have been doing these past nine months. She is a changed person ... and I suppose I've changed a great deal also. Thank you!"

I told the girl's mother that her daughter had <u>learned</u> something about Rational Thinking and that she had made the effort to apply it to her personal life. I assured her that I had done nothing whatsoever <u>to</u> her daughter. It is up to <u>her</u> to do something to and for herself, I concluded. And, it seems that she is.

Food For Thought

- Some people say that death is a tragedy. Others have said it is a blessing. Sometimes death is celebrated. Other times death is mourned. What makes the difference?
- When deaths have occurred in your family or circle of friends, how have you defined them differently? What was different about the events?
- When you think about the people closest to you, how do you imagine their deaths will impact you? Is there a difference in how you define their inevitable deaths?

- Is there something sensible you can do <u>now</u> to better prepare yourself for these events in your life?

<u>ANALYSIS OF ATTITUDES</u>

"Yes, I have had deaths in my family and we define them differently. When a death occurs, we tend to mourn, and be sad. My whole family gets together and everyone starts to drink and talk about the person that just passed away. When I think about the people closest to me, and then imagine them passing away, I think it will have a great impact on me. I cannot imagine losing someone close to me. Yes, there is something sensible I can do to better prepare myself for such an event. I could not take the death so hard. I could look at it as though they are in a better place."

Many books have been written on this subject. First, I believe I must understand that <u>everything</u> that lives will die. There is no question in my mind about that fact. You are going to die someday and so am I. I can "imagine it" happening to us all. I want to face the reality of life and the reality of death. I do not want to pretend that death is never going to happen.

I can imagine losing someone close to me. I had a son that was stillborn. I lost one of my dearest male friends to vodka. My grandparents have all died, as have my aunts and uncles. My favorite college professors are no longer alive. My cousin, David, died recently at an early age. Death is no stranger to me. It is a fact of life.

Yes, "there IS something YOU can do" to better prepare yourself for reality. You can enjoy your family TODAY, while they are alive. You can treat them TODAY like you are not going to be with them tomorrow. You can learn to SHARE with them like you have been unable to do in your past. You can LOVE them as you have refused to love them before. You can ENJOY today with no promise of tomorrow. And, when they die, you can be GRATEFUL for the time you have spent with them.

If you participate in the lives of those you love TODAY, you will have less to mourn when they are no longer here with you.

Think about the realities of life. Enjoy the living. Rejoice in the present. Face reality.

Doc

— — —

"If someone in my immediate family dies I don't know how I would act. I would be lost. I know that's not what you want to hear, but that's how I feel."

We can wait for death to surprise us, or we can think about death and make some decisions that can affect our behavior. For example, you say that if death occurred to an immediate family member, YOU would be LOST. I have counseled with many people who have had immediate family members who died unexpectedly. Sooner or later they walked into my office and said, "You know what? I have suffered enough! It is TIME for me to move on with my life." And, they do. THEY make the conscious decision that enough personal suffering has taken place, and they decide to enjoy life once again.

I have an image for you. Imagine someone you love very much dies and you were not prepared. You are surprised and shocked! Now what? Imagine they are sitting on a cloud, with a beautiful, blue sky all around. They are looking down at you. You happen to be looking up into the sky as they are looking down at you. For a brief moment you can talk to your loved one. What do you think your loved one would share with you?

Would he or she say, "I like the way you are behaving? You are acting depressed, you are drinking too much alcohol, and you are missing work. Those are all good things to do because I am no longer with you. I know that you even considered killing yourself because I am no longer alive. I am so very proud of you!" Of course your loved one would not respond in this way.

So then you ask, "How long do you want me to act sad and lost?" What would you tell your loved one if you were the one who had died? Not so long ago, I asked 1,000 seniors in high school, "How long should you act mournful if someone you love dies? How long should it be obvious to others around you that you are suffering from your loss?" Interesting enough, almost everyone agreed that they should be "obviously mournful" for at least a year. That means that we have <u>learned</u> that obvious suffering after the death of a loved one ought to last at least a year. So if something unforeseen happens that I don't want to happen, I have <u>not suffered enough</u>. The suffering ought to <u>continue</u> for at least a year.

So you say, "Well then, are you suggesting I act happy when someone dies?" No! I am not suggesting that. That would be a little strange, but I am suggesting that YOU have CHOICES about how you think, feel and act when anything in your life happens, including death. You can CHOOSE to be miserable as long as you CHOOSE. You can decide you have suffered enough when you CHOOSE. One person learns to mourn death, another celebrates death. Those are LEARNED responses.

The most important point is that you do NOT have to be LOST when a death occurs. You can read, think and talk about death NOW. It is a part of life, you know. And, I don't want you to experience any more misery in your life than is absolutely necessary, especially if there is something YOU can do about it.

Talk with other friends and loved ones about life AND death. See what others think and how they deal with the ideas. I believe it will make the actual experience more understandable and tolerable for you.

I wish you peace,

Doc

– – –

"I think you should let your friends and families know how you feel about them while they are alive. You never know what can happen."

There seems to be good reasons to spend quality time with your significant others while they are alive. Enjoy the moment.

I rented a room from a man and woman in Westerville, Ohio while I went to undergraduate school. They had a dream. They wanted to spend 2 weeks in Florida together when the husband, a mailman, retired. They saved, dreamed about, and talked about their 2 weeks in Florida when

Ben retired from the post office. Unfortunately, Ben died several months before his retirement date. His wife would not go to Florida with friends! She could not go with her husband as planned. She was determined to never go there.

That was one of many lessons I've learned about when to enjoy my life. I learned, "The time is now!" Life is to be enjoyed everyday. Enjoy life today and there will be nothing to regret tomorrow.

I think you are on the right track.

Doc

– – –

"When I think of my mother dying, I can't stand the fact that she will no longer be with me."

Oh yes you can, and you will. You can and will stand your mother no longer being alive. And, it might be well for you to face the fact today.

You don't want her to die until YOU are ready. But she will die when she dies. You and I do not know when that will be. It may be a surprise or it may be expected. But, she will die, as will you and I. You told me that when your grandma died you "handled it well. She was old, sick and in pain." You thought "she was in a better place now." So there are "conditions" under which death is "acceptable" to you, right? I bet it would be helpful to both you and your mom if you talked to her about your fears and concerns surrounding life and death. Often, people older than us have much different perspectives on life and death. Their opinions and advice can be very eye-opening and growthful to understand. I bet you will be happy you talked with her.

Peace,

Doc

– – –

THIS ISN'T REALLY HAPPENING TO ME!

They came into my office on Sunday afternoon to talk to me. They had talked to me almost two years ago when their daughter was twelve, now she is fourteen. They could not control her behavior when she was twelve and that had not changed. "She is, if anything, getting along with her brother somewhat better after two years of individual counseling, but everything else is just about the same or worse!" Her father said that he "wanted to knock her teeth out just last week!" The reason was that "she seldom talks to me, and when she does she uses such foul language and calls me such foul names that I just about cannot stand it! I would have punched her in the mouth but she is wearing several thousand dollars worth of braces that I had just purchased for her!"

Their daughter does not come home when she is asked. "Just a week ago, several boys in their late teens came to the house to see her. We did not know the boys and our daughter did not introduce them to us. It was 10 p.m. and she said that she just wanted to walk around the block with them." Her dad told her to be home in an hour. Thinking that she would probably not return home on time her dad told the four boys that he wanted them to make sure that his daughter was home in an hour. They agreed to have her home as expected.

Two hours later it was midnight and her father decided to go looking for his daughter. He could not find her but he found the home of one of the boys. He learned that his daughter was "down at the river with the other boys." He found the boys, blamed them for not having his daughter at home and told them to never be seen around his house again. He was "very angry at them."

How do we get this way? What was the daughter's responsibility? Where was she supposed to be and whose responsibility is it?

"She is very defiant when we ask her to do anything," her mother said. "She gets more and more hostile all the time! She seldom talks to me unless she wants something from me. She demands, rather than asks, and she gets furious if I say no. Recently I said no to her and she went into her bedroom and trashed it! She smashed and broke most of what was in there. She was really on a rampage! We asked her psychologist what we should do and he said that our daughter needed some love and understanding. So, we tried not to make a big deal of what she had done to her room. We just left it that way until she cleaned it herself...that was a long time later, however! Her anger and her manipulation are somewhat new these past few years but really I don't believe that it could be drug abuse!"

"So what do you think is behind your daughter's behavior? Why is she acting like this?" I asked.

"We really are not sure," said her father, "but we don't believe that it's drugs. The psychologist says that we need to love her more and be more understanding, but I am not sure how to be understanding about what she is doing, or how to love her more."

"Recently my wife and I went away for the weekend and left our daughter at home. When we came back on Sunday night we found the windshield on our second car had been smashed. We asked our daughter if she knew what happened and she said she had not seen the damage. We called the police and they were unable to determine what had happened. Several weeks later we learned that our daughter and her friend had spent the night together at our home. They wanted some cigarettes and could not buy their own. They knew I smoked and kept a carton under the seat of the car. They could not find the keys to the car so they smashed in the front window with a brick to get my cigarettes. When they got into the car they 'were so angry that they slashed the seats with a knife.' But I really do not think that drugs are involved!"

"So what do you think is behind your daughter's behavior . . . why do you think she would do such things? Is she perhaps insane, or could her insane behavior come from chemical abuse?" I asked.

Her dad went on to tell me how he found his 14-year-old daughter in the back seat of a car with three young men. "They had her undressed and they were playing with her," he said. I almost killed those boys! I wanted to kill them and something stopped me! I could not believe what they were doing to my daughter! As I attempted to stop them my daughter called me names that I seldom have heard. She said that I should go away and let her alone. She said that she knew what she was doing. She fought me, kicking and screaming, as I forced her into my car to take her home. The boys ran away the first chance they had and my daughter was furious with me. I hated those young men!"

How did we ever get this way, I asked myself. How do we look past what our children are doing and blame someone else? Is it that we have to blame ourselves when our children do not live up to our expectations? Is our children's behavior our fault?

"Yes, sure, my daughter has a beer now and then! Once she got a little drunk with some of her girlfriends at a party and we had to go and get her. That does not mean that she had a drug problem!" said her father. "You know kids will be kids and perhaps it is just a stage my daughter is going through. My wife and I have discussed it and we think that by the time she graduates from high school she will have grown out of this behavior," he said.

What if she kills herself in the meantime? What if she gets in the backseat of a car with three young men and you don't find her? Who is responsible for your daughter's behavior?" I asked again. "Are you, her parents, responsible for what she does? Are you willing to follow her around for the rest of her teenage years, attempting to correct her mistakes while feeling guilty for what she has done? That is a tremendous responsibility!"

"Well, perhaps it is just a phase that she is going through," said her mother. "Although recently we had some friends visit and we mixed some cocktails for them. When my husband's friend took a sip of his drink he kidded us because the drink was 'all water with no liquor.' My husband said that he had mixed it like he knew he liked it. His friend said that my husband should taste the drink. There was no liquor in the drink, for there was no liquor in the bottle. The liquor in the cabinet was all gone. Someone had emptied the bottles and filled them with colored water! We could not believe that someone would think that we were that stupid. But, we want you to know that we do not think it was our daughter. We just cannot believe that drugs are a problem in this case!" her mother said again.

"Our daughter has been making failing grades in school for the past several semesters. She has been skipping school and forging notes from us to her counselor. We are very concerned that she will have to repeat a grade and will not graduate from high school on schedule. We just cannot understand what has brought about this behavior change. She used to be so very different," her dad said softly.

"Have you had her to a physician recently? Perhaps there is something physically wrong with your daughter that is causing these problems?" I suggested.

"Yes, we took her to our family doctor and he said there was nothing wrong with her physically. He was the one that suggested that we bring her to the Outreach Program for treatment," said her dad.

"But Outreach is a drug abuse rehabilitation center for adolescents. Why would he suggest bringing her here if there is no drug problem?"

"I think she could have a problem like that," said her mom. "My husband does not agree with me. It just seems impossible that drugs could be the problem!"

"You know," her mom, continued, "I wanted to take my daughter to the mall last weekend to have lunch and shop for the day. My daughter said that she did not want to go with me. When I asked her why, she said that she did not want her friends to see her with me. That really hurt! I just do not know what could have done this to my daughter."

"Well, what do you suppose could have changed your daughter into this strange, angry, manipulative, hateful, resentful, foul-mouthed young person? Could it be that 'the devil made her do it'? Could it be that she has some 'mental problem'? Could it be a Communist plot to overthrow your family? What could be wrong? Is it not possible that chemicals have come into your child's life and have altered her behavior, her attitudes and her emotions? They can do that, you know. If it were a drug problem, then it would not be your fault. It could be a relief to find out that drugs are responsible for these changes in your daughter's behavior. We can treat chemical abuse. We can teach you how to help your child get un-abused by drugs and you can have your family back together once again. That is something worth considering."

Why couldn't the parents of this young girl understand what seemed very clear to me? Why were they choosing to close their eyes to what was going on? Would they have to suffer shame and guilt if they learned that their daughter had a mind of her own and that she can get into trouble with drugs even when her parents are doing the best they know how to do?

The father interrupted my thoughts. He said, "But we could not bring our daughter into treatment at this time because she would miss the end of her eighth year in school."

"But I thought you said she was skipping school and failing the eighth grade?" I questioned.

"Well, she is, but she might luck-out and pass anyway," her dad responded.

"Ah yes, I forgot for a moment that 'passing' is what we are interested in, not learning," I said.

"Anyway," her mother went on, "we have such a fun summer planned that we would not want any of the family to miss any of the vacation."

"Help me to understand why you are interested in entertaining the daughter that calls you filthy names and makes you drive your car in search of her in the middle of the night?"

"I guess that we just love her and want her to have a nice summer," her dad said. "It would be just awful if we brought her to Outreach for treatment and found she was not doing drugs. She might never speak to us again! I mean all that we know is that she has had a couple of beers in her life."

"She is fourteen years old! Were you drinking 'a couple of beers' and needing to be picked up from parties because you had too much to drink when you were fourteen? Were you calling your dad filthy names and did he want to knock your teeth out because of your language? Did you act like your daughter at age fourteen?"

"Well no!" said the dad, "but then, times are different now."

"So because times are different, you two have to be out of control with your daughter? You have to resort to wondering where she is at night. You have to wonder who is drinking your liquor without your permission. You have to wonder who breaks into your car to steal cigarettes. Is that how different it is today, or is it that alcohol and other drugs have changed your daughter's behavior to the point that you are all out of control?"

Her dad said, "You have really been kind to us. I think that we had better go home and think about what you have said, but I want to state again that we don't think that our daughter has a drug problem. I am just afraid that if we do something right now we might ruin her passing the eighth grade and ruin her summer vacation and she might never forgive us for that!"

"I don't blame you for being concerned parents. You and your daughter have a serious problem and you *all* need some professional help for sure. You came to a drug abuse rehabilitation center twice for advice and I really wonder why you did that. I believe that you suspect that your daughter has a drug problem but it seems too horrible to admit to yourself. You think that you could not withstand the shame that would go with the admission."

"Remember that you did not do drugs with your child. You did not buy drugs for your child. You did not recommend drug abuse to your child. You did not force your child to smoke cigarettes or drink alcohol. Perhaps her peers did that, but you did not. Her use or abuse is her fault and that is not your fault. You do not have the power to stop your daughter's insane behavior, and you could get the credit for saving her life! Your daughter would not like your taking charge, but she will appreciate your help when she is straight once again."

"Once my son got very angry at me for taking him to our family physician when he had an internal infection. He did not like shots and he saw no necessity to have one. I took him kicking and screaming because

I knew that I was doing something that was in his best interest. You are facing the same thing. Your daughter is out of control from your point of view and from her own. Why else would she treat herself and you in this manner? Admit her to treatment because she needs it, not because she wants it!"

"It just seems like the wrong time to me, Dr. Brown! I want to give her more time to straighten herself out," her dad said.

"I understand that you are struggling with denial right now. I understand that when you faced your daughter for the first time in the nursery of the hospital where she was born you never once imagined her in a drug abuse center at age fourteen. I know that you would rather go on a happy family summer vacation than come into treatment at Outreach. Any sane parent would rather go on a happy summer vacation than go to drug counseling. I also know a family that would not face the fact that their child needed help and she is dead today from driving under the influence of drugs. I know another family that avoided treatment for their child and he shot himself to death while under the influence of drugs. Drugs allow humans to do things they would never do if drugs were not in their bodies. Please look at what is going on in your daughter's life and within your family. It looks to me like drugs are controlling lots of behaviors and you think that is too painful to admit."

"The moment you admit that drugs are a problem in your family is the moment that recovery will begin for all of you.

"Drugs have changed your family. You need to get drugs out of your family and restore it to sanity. I know you do not want to hear this, but I would be less than caring if I told you what you wanted to hear."

The parents thanked me for my time and left the office.

How do I reach people that are so very afraid of seeing what is right in front of them? How do I help parents to understand that children have minds of their own, they do what they want?

How did we get this way?

---DENIAL!

Food For Thought

- Our children have minds of their own. They may do what <u>they</u> want, not necessarily what <u>we</u> want. When they do what <u>they</u> want, what does that say about us, their parents?
- Are we capable of making sure our children follow in <u>our</u> footsteps? Can we insure they adopt our values, morals and preferences?
- Being best friends to our children is a popular role for many parents. "If I take exception to my sons' or daughters' plans and desires, they may never speak to me again. I cannot take that risk!" What role are you playing as a parent? How might you be more effective after reading this story? Please be specific.

THE NIGHT AFTER THANKSGIVING

So who's in charge?

I am!

What do you mean?

What do you mean, what do you mean? I am in charge of *my* life and the way that I *think*!

Tonight as my wife and I sat on our back patio, enjoying the cool Florida weather, the married couple in the rented house behind us was swearing at one another, screaming and breaking things in their house. She screamed, "F--k you, I'm leaving!" Then there was more pounding, more screaming and more swearing.

They were each *controlling* the other and they were both *hurting* each other. Someone was *in charge* of the pain! Who was it?

I blamed the male voice. I wanted to take charge, dial 9-1-1 and have someone stop the pain. I wanted to rescue the *helpless* female. I wanted to take the world in *my* hands and protect the victim in the situation.

But, *who* is the *helpless* victim? Perhaps it is the one that *thinks* he or she is helpless.

Is *she* helpless? Hell no! She just *thinks* she is helpless.

She is as *powerful* as she wants to be. She does not have to suffer at the hands of a man who wants to control her. She screamed, "I'm leaving!" And then, she stayed, to fight, long into the night, and the next day.

She *thinks* she deserves to be hurt? Her father hurt her mother and now a man is hurting her. That's how she makes sense of it all, that's how she continues to endure the suffering. "If it was good enough for my mother, it's good enough for me!"

She refuses to think beyond what she has seen in her past. Her mother got beaten and now she gets beaten. What else is there for her?

The fact is that *she* puts up with only that which *she* decides to put up with.

I know better than to ever even think of hitting my wife! Marcia believes that she was *not* meant to be hurt and therefore she is *not* going to stand for such treatment.

So what's the difference?

The difference is in our *attitudes* and *beliefs*!

I've heard that since I was a little boy! People told me to *change my attitude!* They told me that *my attitude was the problem*, <u>not</u> what was happening to me. They said that my <u>attitude</u> was controlling my behavior, not the environment!

Tonight, I'd bet a dollar that the problem is *her husband*.

She thinks *she has to take it* and therefore she stays for more abuse.

She's got a *stinking* attitude for she does not have to stay. She does not have to be abused.

She has a *choice*. She has lots of choices.

Who is going to tell her? Who is she going to believe? Who can make her listen and understand? Why hasn't she listened before? What is wrong with her attitude that she cannot hear, or will not hear?

Why do I care? Why do I upset myself because she won't live like I want her to live?

I have made a living, for the past 30 years, suggesting to men, women, boys and girls, that *we all have choices* about how we are treated and what we must put up with in life. We have <u>choices</u>, lots of choices.

We do not have to endure *shitty situations* that we do not want to endure! Is that news to you?

<u>We have choices about what we do and what we think!</u>

We are *powerful* human beings and we <u>can</u> make powerful choices! We <u>can</u> get out of abusive situations! We <u>can</u> protect ourselves, care for ourselves, or offer ourselves to others to be abused.

It is uncomfortable to change! That is a neurological fact. Change brings conflict. That's a fact. But, have you ever thought that change can be *less* painful than staying where you are?

Oh the hell with it! You won't listen! You say that I *cannot understand because I am not in your situation.*

So stay where you are and suffer some more!

Just remember, one day when the pain gets really intense, that *you do not have to stay where you are and hurt! There are, whether you know it or not, other people in the world who will love you, care for you, and treat you with kindness, respect and gentleness, if you care enough about yourself to look for them. Give them a chance to find you.*

You take a risk staying where you are. Take a rational risk and get out!

Stop hating yourself!

Start loving yourself!

Change your *attitude* and change your behavior.

Someday soon you will thank yourself.

Change is possible. Happiness is possible. Love is possible. Love and happiness can come to you if you make yourself available.

Do it *differently* tonight, please.

Food For Thought

- "If I try harder I think I can get him to stop drinking! Perhaps there is something I am doing to make him like this. I can't give up now!" How are you in charge of how someone else behaves?
- Henry Ford said, "If you think you can't, you can't. If you think you can, you can!" Even The Little Engine That Could said, "I think I can, I think I can." And, he did! What is it that you think you can't? Do you suppose you really could?
- Do you suppose your ability to change can really come from thinking differently? Can simply the notion of, "I think I can," really make a significant difference?

ANALYSIS OF ATTITUDES

"I have little or no control over what other people do. I can only control myself. But, I really don't think I can stop smoking. I have tried a million times. If I thought "I could stop smoking," that might just give me the extra push I need to be successful. If I don't believe in myself, then how can I expect others to believe in me?"

Smoking cessation is an important topic and one that I have discussed many times in this book. Perhaps you've already found some help by reading previous stories. For sure, you haven't "tried a million times" to STOP. And, if indeed you have, then the millionth-and-one time might just do the trick, especially if this time YOU thought, "I CAN BE SUCCESSFUL!"

You are so right, YOU must BELIEVE in YOU! YOU started smoking and YOU CAN STOP! YOU are able to control what YOU put in your mouth. YOU can remember when YOU were a NON-smoker and YOU can become a NON-smoker again, whenever YOU choose.

I invite you to join me today, as a NON-smoker.

Doc

— — —

"MOM" NELSON

It was Orientation Week at Otterbein College in central Ohio. The new freshman class had come to campus a week early to move into the dorms, learn the layout of the campus, be rushed by fraternity and sorority actives, meet their professors and register for classes. It was an exciting and anxious time for each and every new freshman.

The fraternity parties, new dorm friends and trips to a local college hangout were the most impressive. There was also the young freshman majorette in the cafeteria line that made quite an impression on me as I remember. She was 5'2" tall, had short blonde hair, with large, round, blue eyes, and she was very outgoing indeed. Somehow I managed to always be right behind her in line for each and every breakfast, lunch and dinner. She was not only pretty, she seemed most interested in my attention. That only seemed to reinforce the idea that I wanted to be where ever she was during those ten days of orientation. Not to mention the fact that the upperclassmen had warned me that as soon as the rest of the college students reported to campus, the freshman would no longer have any chance with the pretty coeds. The competition would be too much for us to stand.

Those days seemed far away at the moment.

There was a meeting in an hour in the Chapel with the Dean of Students. It was to be a State of the Union Address. The Dean was stern, although he did his best to welcome us to our new college life. He said that the admission's standards were a bit relaxed in that it was "easier to be admitted than it was to graduate." In fact he said that, "by Christmas, only one-third of those in attendance in Chapel that day would remain. The rest of the Freshman Class would be sent home because of poor academic performance." We had one semester to prove ourselves to those in power! I will never forget the Dean asking us to "look at the person on our right, and then look at the person on your left. Two of you will not be here after the Holidays!" That was not an exciting piece of news to ponder.

I had to wonder if I would be one of the fortunate people to still be on campus when the year ended.

One new friend, and impressive fraternity active, was a man named "Ruble." He sure seemed to know what was going on. He had lots of advice about almost every subject and he was willing to share it with any young freshman that would listen. He was clear about one issue. He said that Freshman English Composition was the course that was used to "weed out the Freshman Class!" And in particular, there was one professor who seemed to enjoy that process more than any other. Her name was Mrs. Margaret Nelson, not so affectionately known as "Mom." Ruble warned me to "stay away from her. And, at all cost, not to register for her English class!"

The last Saturday of Orientation Week was Registration Day. It took place in the campus gym. It was called a "scramble situation" in which the students came to the gym, en masse', and when the doors opened it was a free-for-all. Students went in all directions to line up in front of the professors they most wanted to take classes from, and then waited in line to see if they could get registered before the classes filled up and therefore closed.

I wanted to major in mathematics and minor in physics. I had heard of a couple of men who were especially talented in those areas and so I went straight to their lines. The lines were not as long as other's, for math was not as particularly popular a subject. Nevertheless, it took time to register for the courses that led to my major. And, worse than that, I forgot about the warnings from "Ruble" about "Mom" Nelson.

All of a sudden an immobilizing fear took over my body. I looked in the direction of the English Department lines and the Freshman English Composition Courses were all filled, with the exception of one. Mrs. Nelson was the only professor remaining with room for me!

Now that might not have been as bad as it appeared, but I did not have an impressive track record in English. For the best part of twelve years of public education, I had been told time and time again, that my handwriting was sloppy at best, that my spelling was not at all impressive, and that I could not write themes to acceptable academic levels. That past feedback, coupled now with thoughts of sitting in Mrs. Nelson's English class, made my feet feel very heavy indeed as I attempted to approach the desk where she was seated.

I really didn't want to be one of the two-thirds of the student body that would be leaving at the end of the first semester!

I finally approached Mrs. Nelson's desk and explained that, "I wanted to take her course." She was rather business-like as she signed my registration form and said, "I will see you Monday morning at 7:45, Mr. Brown."

Well Monday morning came and I walked into Mrs. Nelson's class before the required 7:45 a.m. bell. She was seated at her desk and seemed to watch each of us as we chose a place to spend the hour. When all the students were seated, Mrs. Nelson closed the door and stood before us. She explained once again that this course was going to teach some of us how to become more proficient writers as well as weed out some of the less fortunate students. I was more nervous than ever before!

Then it happened! Mrs. Nelson explained that she wanted to get better acquainted with how well we could express ourselves on paper. "I want you to write a theme for me. Do the best job that you know how to do. I want you to write a theme about the most important character you have ever met. It is due on Friday!"

I clearly remember thinking that this might possibly be the last college theme I would ever be asked to write!

Friday came and my theme was complete. I chose to write about the coed that I met in the cafeteria line. I wrote about how exciting it was to meet a lovely creature such as she. She looked absolutely beautiful in the morning while waiting in line for breakfast. Her light blonde hair reflected the morning sun as though it was covered with diamond dust. And most importantly, I felt simply grand when she turned around, looked into my eyes, and said, "I was hoping you would find me here again this morning!" She was magical! I shared her, on paper, with Mrs. Nelson.

I handed in my theme. Mrs. Nelson explained that she had time to read the papers over the weekend and we could expect to get them returned to us on Monday morning.

Monday morning came. I appeared in class at 7:45 as expected. Mrs. Nelson handed back all the papers except one. I did not receive a theme! I raised my hand and said, "Mrs. Nelson, my name is David Brown, and I did not receive a theme from you?" Mrs. Nelson was quick to respond. She replied, "I want to see you personally after class!" Her face appeared stern and her voice seemed to lack any sign of warmth. I was very concerned, but also somehow relieved to realize that she was going to be critical of me privately.

I expected the worst!

After my peers had left the room, I approached Mrs. Nelson's Desk. She asked me be seated in the chair next to her desk. She took my paper out of a folder on her desk. She looked at the paper for a moment and then looked directly into my eyes. I will never forget the words she then spoke.

Mrs. Nelson said, "It had been many years since I have read such a theme! I wept when I read your thoughts regarding the young woman that you met during Orientation. You have a gift, David. You write beautifully. You gave me reason to believe that I was right there with you and your new friend. I was able to feel what you were feeling through your description. I asked another English professor to read your theme, and he agreed with me. You have a talent for writing."

I could hardly believe my ears. It was I, David Brown. I had impressed Mrs. Nelson with my writing. I could indeed write!

Since that very moment I have enjoyed writing.

Mrs. Nelson and I became grand friends. I worked hard to impress her even more with my work and she knew how to draw the effort out of me. She was the gifted person in the story indeed.

I wondered after graduation from college, if Mrs. Nelson somehow knew that I needed to hear something positive about myself, and talked to me as she did to motivate me, or did she really mean what she said. I suppose it didn't really matter. She had indeed made a very significant impression on me.

Thank you kindly, Mrs. Nelson!

Food For Thought

· Positive encouragement can be a powerful force in our lives. Was there a "Mom Nelson" in your life?
· What impact did her encouragement have on your life?
· Did you ever have the chance to thank your "Mom Nelson?" Perhaps it's not too late.

ANALYSIS OF ATTITUDES

"My 'Mom' Nelson was Mrs. Edwards. She was my eighth grade English/Literature teacher. She was the dreaded English teacher that students disliked because her class was difficult. I quickly learned that Mrs. Edwards wasn't an evil person but an exceptional and caring teacher. I loved to read (and still do) and she encouraged my reading and opened doors for me to Shakespeare, Dickens and Steinbeck. She taught me how to write, do research and use proper grammar. Mrs. Edward's positive encouragement and exceptional teaching skills helped me breeze through high school and has helped me a lot since starting college. Mrs. Edwards passed away in 1991. She was my best friend and mentor for the ten years I knew her. She is still helping me today."

Congratulations! An outstanding teacher is a thing of beauty and a joy forever.

Doc

– – –

"Actually, I had a 'Mom" Nelson and an "Anti-Mom" Nelson. My "Anti-Mom" Nelson was my 4th grade math teacher. On one of her "pop-quizzes" I scored an "F." I never had an "F" before in math. When I picked up my quiz from my teacher, she said, "Oh…you have an 'F,' you are not good at math! Maybe you are good in other courses, but not math." For the next 2 years I had trouble with math. I believed I was not good enough. But then, everything changed. I met my new math teacher, Carmen Palacios. She told our class she wanted us to learn all we could, and then some. At the end of the year, she told me, "You have an extraordinary ability to solve math problems. You are very good with numbers. I am proud of you. Please continue to take math courses." Since then I love math."

Teachers' words can carry such power in them. We look to others for our worth and value. We do better when we are encouraged, and we can give up when told to do so. Our self-concepts are supposed to be built on what WE tell OURSELVES, but often they are constructed on the words of others.

I am so happy you had a "Mom" Nelson to overcome the "Anti-Mom" Nelson.

Peace,

Doc

– – –

"Yes, I also had a "Mom" Nelson. She encouraged me to, "Go for it!" in life. She always encouraged me to do my best. She made me believe I could do anything I put my mind to doing. I have thanked her many times for her help and guidance."

Remember, she was only encouraging you to do what she believed possible for you. You are capable of giving yourself the same, strong, positive encouragement. Go for it!

Doc

– – –

KIM

Southeastern Arizona was a new and wonderful place in which to live. I moved there from Cleveland, Ohio after the completion of a Master's Degree in Counseling. It was hard to believe that there was a place to live where the sun shown almost 360 days a year. The weather was warm and sunny, and the air was clean and fresh. It was simply glorious!

I moved to Arizona to help develop a new college in the desert. The college was located in the desert between two towns, one town was eight miles away and the other was twelve miles from the campus. The college was eight miles from the Mexican border. Forty miles east of the campus lay the Chiricahua Mountains, the former home of Cochise and Geronimo and the Chiricahua Apaches.

The Chiricahua Mountains rose 11,000 feet and were a great attraction to me. When it was 80 degrees at the college we could drive to the mountains and sled ride in the snow at 8,500 feet. Cleveland did not have scenery like this part of the country and the diverse terrain seemed amazing to me.

The mountains were also home to a rather interesting man. He was the "world's leading authority on spiders" and he was employed by the Museum of Natural History. He and his wife lived at, and operated, the research station in the Chiricahua Mountains. I was fascinated to meet Vince because I could not imagine what "the world's leading authority on spiders" might look like.

You see, in Cleveland we had only one kind of spider that I recall. They were called "Daddy Long-Legs," and were about as harmless a creature as one might find. One could not harm me if it chewed on me for an hour. But somehow, I grew up in Cleveland having learned to fear spiders. I didn't like them and did not want to share the same space with them!

I wondered what Vince would be like? Would he be covered with long, black and silver hair like the Arizona tarantula, and might he sleep up in the rafters of the research station, rather than in a comfortable bed? I got my chance to meet Vince and his wife the very first Thanksgiving recess from college. Another staff member and I took 60 students on a retreat from the college to the research station. It was a grand way to experience the mountains as well as meet the spider expert.

Both Vince and his wife were fun people to meet. They were very familiar with the out-of-doors, as well as being very hospitable hosts. They taught us a great deal about our temporary home. They also shared their travels with us as they had traveled all over the world searching for, and collecting, spiders to bring back to Arizona for their museum collection.

The research station contained literally thousands and thousands of both live and preserved spiders from around the world. They certainly came in all colors, shapes and sizes. It very much interested me to learn that Vince was spending his life collecting spiders. He seemed so normal. He was a pleasure to meet and study with.

We learned that Vince and his wife had plans to adopt a Korean girl. In fact, Vince was to fly to Los Angeles the day before Thanksgiving to meet his new daughter for the first time. He was going to bring her back to Arizona and both he and Kim would arrive at the research station on Thanksgiving Day. This added to the excitement of the holiday for all of us!

There was quite a bit of discussion about Kim and her arrival. Vince and his wife spoke no Korean, and Kim was reported to speak no English. That presented a problem from the very beginning. Vince and his wife, living in a fur trader's cabin at the research station, decided that they would do what the early Indians and white men used to do. They would give Kim a gift, the universal symbol for friendship. We all talked about what they ought to give their new five-year-old daughter upon her arrival in the mountains. Many items were suggested.

The day before Thanksgiving arrived and Vince left for California. The activities of the retreat continued. The weather at 8,000 feet was cold. The snow had accumulated to more than a foot. The mountains were a wonderfully beautiful place to spend the Thanksgiving Holiday after leaving the warmth of the desert below.

We all started to help prepare for the Thanksgiving dinner. There was a lot of work to be done with almost one hundred people expected for dinner. It was a personal thrill for me to be in Arizona, in the mountains, with sixty college students, and the staff from the research station. What a celebration we were having. And soon, there would be a new member of the family arriving from the other side of the world.

The students and staff worked very well together and soon it was time to eat the results of our collective efforts. Thanksgiving dinner was on the tables and people were starting to pass around the large bowls of food. Just as the eating started, the main doors to the dining room opened, and in walked Vince and Kim.

Everyone in the room looked in their direction, rose to their feet and applauded. Kim somehow seemed to know that <u>she</u> was the guest of honor for she grinned as wide as any little girl has ever grinned. It was indeed an exciting moment for all of us.

Vince and Kim joined us at the feast, and we all ate far past the point of sensibility. It was the best Thanksgiving dinner ever!

As the pie and coffee were being served, it was suggested that Vince give Kim her "welcome to the family" present. Vince was eager to comply. He left the room for a moment, and when he returned, he was carrying a small present with a very large bow. The box was about one foot square. He placed the package in front of Kim and motioned to her that the present was for her.

It appeared that Kim did not need to be told. She knew what a present was and she began to remove the brightly colored paper. Inside the paper was a terrarium. It was a glass box containing one of Vince's favorite possessions ... a ten-year-old, female, Arizona, tarantula spider!

Students began to leave the dining room in all directions! No one asked anyone's permission, they just left!

I was shocked! I could not believe my eyes. "Why would this rational, kind, gentle man give this beautiful young child such a dangerous creature?" I could hardly believe my eyes! Vince removed the top of the glass box and took Kim's hand. He guided her right hand, palm up, into the top of the box. The spider began to climb onto her hand and up her wrist.

Kim beamed! She smiled a big smile. She looked pleased. Vince seemed to be very happy that his new daughter appeared happy with her gift. I continued to be very uncomfortable with what I was watching!

I could no longer contain myself! I asked Vince how it was possible for him to give Kim such a dangerous pet. He looked at me and smiled. He asked if I was serious. I said I was indeed serious. How could he do such a thing to his new daughter?

Vince explained that Kim's new pet was as dangerous as the creatures that flew through the air in Ohio, where I was born. He was talking about the ones that landed on human's bodies and sucked out their blood while injecting a toxin into their skin. They caused itching and welts and were a constant irritation in the summer. He was referring to mosquitoes. Vince explained that the spider was not a killer and that it was not dangerous to Kim. He said that one day Kim would squeeze the spider too hard or irritate it somehow and the spider would indeed bite her. She would get a small welt that would itch, and Kim would learn how to treat the spider so as not to be bitten again.

Vince picked up the spider and handed it to me. He asked me to hold it. I could not! I was afraid. I learned as a youngster that spiders were bad and not to be handled. Even though Vince said the spider could not hurt me I could not touch it.

I thought about it through the night. I believed Vince when he said the spider could not hurt me. I had learned to trust his word. I outweighed the spider by 180 pounds. It was really no threat to me, but my fear kept me away from it. It held all the power for the moment.

I decided to not let the spider win this contest. There was no rational reason to fear something that could not hurt me. I went to the research station lab the next morning and found Kim's spider. I put it on a lab table and placed my hand near the creature. It did not attack me! I placed my hand in the path of the spider and allowed it to walk over one of my fingers … then two fingers … and then my whole hand. I survived the experience!

The more I allowed the spider to touch me the more my fear seemed to subside. By talking to myself about the reality of the spider, while touching and surviving the experience, the less fearful I became. Therein was the lesson. By attacking my fear, by doing exactly what it was I was most afraid to do, and talking to myself about the reality of the situation, that being that the spider was not going to harm me, the fear was subsiding.

Perhaps Kim thought about the spider as an American child might think of a gerbil. They are cute, playful, fuzzy, entertaining, loveable, and friendly. If I had grown up to think of spiders in the same manner, then I would have understood Vince's gift to his new daughter and certainly would not have been afraid.

Dr. Carl Rogers, the world-renowned psychologist, said years ago, that it is not reality that controls how human beings behave, but rather perceived reality. Reality is not our guiding light. It is our view of reality that shapes our behavior.

His theory certainly held true in this case.

Food For Thought

- Do spiders have the ability to scare humans, or do some humans scare themselves about spiders? What's the difference? Why make a distinction about who scares whom?
- Did you ever have a fear that you overcame? How, specifically, did you do it?
- What advice can you share with someone else about overcoming fear?

ANALYSIS OF ATTITUDES

"I used to have a fear of riding roller coasters. I used to be scared to death of them. After I got older, my attitude changed. I realized there was nothing to be afraid of and that my fear was silly. It was based on untruths about roller coasters. The most important thing I can do to overcome my fear is to change my attitude. It is important that I have an attitude based on facts and positive thinking."

You said it well. Most fear is based on bad information…untruths. When you dealt with what was really going on, your fear went away. I wish you continued success with your new insight.

Doc

— — —

"I was always afraid of being without a partner. I couldn't imagine being alone. Since my son's father and I broke up I haven't been in a serious relationship. I didn't like being alone. I hated it. I hated not having someone. But, I've changed now! I'm not afraid to be alone anymore. I think the best advice I can give someone about overcoming a fear is to face it head-on. I looked at what it was that I believed about being alone. I thought I could not make it alone. That was far from being factual. I was afraid I could not raise a son by myself. That was a false belief also. I have more potential and abilities than I gave myself credit for, and it scared me. When I redefined who I am, my faith in myself greatly increased and my fear disappeared."

Life is beautiful when we see ourselves as capable, powerful people. Congratulations!

Doc

— — —

TOOTSIE POP THERAPY

It was another warm, sunny morning in Southwest Florida, the kind we moved to Florida to enjoy. It was a pleasure just to be alive and headed to a new job.

I was hired to develop a Geriatric-Psychiatry Center for a local hospital, and this was the first day patients were to appear for treatment. The reason for the creation of the Center was that local citizens were in need of assistance. They were elderly, between the ages of 70 and 90, without family members in the area, or had no family members at all for support. They did not cook for themselves and were not getting their minimal daily nutritional requirements for good health. They needed medical care and it was impossible, or inconvenient for them to get to doctors' offices. They were sad or depressed and not seeking help. They lacked companionship and the friendship that they were once accustomed to as younger members of the community.

Neighbors, professionals in the community, and family members, referred the men and women to us. Once we had a group of forty grandmas and grandpas in need of help, we invited them to accept our transportation to the hospital on the first Monday morning of the month. They were going to be evaluated by a team of professionals, including our psychiatrist, social worker, geriatric nurse, and me, a psychologist. Together, our goal was to help each individual experience a happier, healthier existence.

The staff at the Center was excited! It had taken a lot of planning and work to arrive at Opening Day. Looking back, I assumed that we would be met with some eagerness on the part of the patients. We were ready, willing, and able to help. We valued personal health and happiness, and we wanted to share what we knew with those who would listen. Opening Day was an exciting event for the staff!

The bus that the hospital supplied to meet our transportation needs appeared at the entrance to the Center. Almost all the seats were occupied. Our staff met the bus and greeted the new arrivals with smiles and enthusiasm.

The women and men exiting the bus appeared to be less enthusiastic than we were at that moment. However, it was my job to greet them in our new Group Room and to explain our expectations and intentions. I imagined that they were somewhat apprehensive, as anyone might be when trying something new. I was a little apprehensive myself. But, I also imagined, with my skills, I would soon be able to put them at ease and we would get along well.

There were forty men and women in the group. The youngest member was 74 and the eldest was 89. I explained our new program and enthusiastically invited the group members to take an active role in counseling sessions, evaluations, and meals that were being offered. However, it soon became apparent that the members of this group would prefer to have been left alone, and not to have been bothered with traveling to the Center on this Monday morning! I remember feeling somewhat helpless. I asked the group some questions about their lives and activities, and almost none wanted to answer my questions. One man said that he would rather be home, sitting in his chair, staring out the window, waiting to die!

Day One was very difficult indeed! I used my best techniques to get the individuals in the group to talk with me. I offered them my skills and experience in changing their lives and attitudes, just a bit, to make life more enjoyable. I told them that I thought life did not have to hurt, and that I wanted to be a change agent in their lives. No matter what I said, for the most part they seemed not to want to cooperate with me.

Soon the first day was over and the bus took folks back to their homes. The staff spent several hours discussing the day and what we could do differently to get their attention. I remembered thinking of my

Human Behavior classes with Dr. Viktor Frankl. I knew I had to tap into something memorable and positive, if even for a moment.

I remembered Kojak who used to enjoy a Tootsie Pop during times of stress while fulfilling his detective duties. Watching his television show reminded me how good a Tootsie Pop tasted as a youngster. I bought many a bag and took them to my office. I kept them in a jar on my desk and shared them with patients during therapy in my offices in Indiana, and Florida. They were a simple treat for us, and brought back many memories of pleasant times that had gone before. I was seldom, if ever, without those delicious candy suckers in my desk drawer or home pantry.

I was reminded of the power of a Tootsie Pop as I sat at home that day. I drove to my favorite store in the neighborhood and purchased a large, yellow box containing 100 Tootsie Pops. The next morning, after the forty members of my group had been seated in the Group Room, I entered the room to take my seat amongst them. Under my left arm was the yellow box of suckers. I sat down, placed the box on the seat next to me, and began to talk to the group.

I barely got one sentence out of my mouth, when a woman interrupted me, "Are those Tootsie Pops in that box?" I told her they were Tootsie Pops and that I like to keep them in my desk to be enjoyed during the day.

She asked, "Are you going to share them with us?" I said that was not my intention, actually.

She responded, "I have not had a Tootsie Pop since I was a little girl, and I would really like you to share one with me!"

One of the men interrupted her by saying, "I would like one also, but I would like to pick my own flavor!"

Almost without hesitation, various men and women sitting around me made it clear that they each wanted one! The mood of the group was indeed changing, and becoming much more positive.

I agreed to share the Tootsie Pops with the group. But, I wanted something in return. I explained that during the 5 or 10 minutes, while enjoying a Tootsie Pop, I wanted the individual group members to focus on the sweet taste of the sucker and think about memories of when they last enjoyed a Tootsie Pop. They agreed! The yellow box of Tootsie Pops was passed around the circle. Some men and women asked to be able to take two, one for when they were at home that night. I agreed. All forty participants took a sucker. One woman had a serious problem with diabetes and could not eat candy, but she asked to be able to take one anyway, just to have in her purse.

Soon we were all enjoying a Tootsie Pop together. The <u>sounds</u> of enjoying Tootsie Pops were coming from around the room. Smiles were appearing on faces, as the sweet candy brought back positive childhood memories of their last Tootsie Pops. Stories began to be told of instances when we went to the local candy shop, or grocery store, and adults in the family bought us a Tootsie Pop treat. I remembered going to the corner store for the construction workers building homes in our neighborhood. They sent me to the store for cold drinks, and in return, I could keep the soda bottles for the deposit. Most often I used the deposit money to purchase Tootsie Pops, a just reward indeed!

I must say that our Tootsie Pop experience was the turning point for most of the Grandmas and Grandpas in the group. We realized, together, that there <u>are</u> some enjoyable things to be experienced. There were Tootsie Pops, and more!

Once again, Tootsie Pops played a significant role in my professional life, as well as in the lives of the patients with whom I shared them. They have been, and continue to be, a memorable event in the lives of Americans, both young and not so young.

Food For Thought

- Remember those little, multi-colored dots of candy on long, white strips of paper? We ate the dots right off the paper. Do you remember the black, wax mustaches, and the red wax lips that could be worn and then chewed? Remember "Bull's Eyes?" Remember when there were a couple of multi-colored gumballs in the gumball machine, and if you got one of those, you could

149

trade it in for a whole candy bar? How do you feel when you remember?

- The Tootsie Pop has "awesome power," or does it? Is there "power" in the candy sucker, or in the <u>minds</u> of those who remember a positive event in their lives? Most grandmas and grandpas remembered positive events wherein Tootsie Pops were included. One grandma, however, began to cry as she placed the Tootsie Pop in her mouth. She wept as mournfully as anyone I had ever seen! I put my arm around her and inquired as to what she was experiencing. She said, "I am crying because every time my father sexually abused me, he gave me a Tootsie Pop! This sucker brings back so many unhappy memories."

ANALYSIS OF ATTITUDES

"I actually started to smile and laugh to myself while reading this story. I thought about the commercial with the owl who said, "How many licks does it take to get to the center of a Tootsie Pop – one, two – crunch!" It is funny how thinking about candy I have eaten as a child can make me feel happy today."

As you read in this story, memories can make one smile, or memories can make one cry. I am happy to hear that yours were happy-producing memories.

Peace,

Doc

— — —

"I am similar to the grandma that wept. I had a rough childhood with an abusive father. When I think about the candy from my childhood, it brings back the memories of my dad and the things I was trying to get away from while eating candy."

I sincerely hope that you have been able to put the difficulties of your childhood in proper perspective by this time in your life. Sometimes it is very helpful to seek professional help from a licensed, board certified counselor to work through your childhood memories. I thank you for sharing your thoughts with me and wish you only the best in your adult life.

Doc

— — —

"When I was 6 my parents divorced and my life went into a tail spin. My dad moved back to his small hometown and I visited each weekend. He married a horrible woman. The good thing though was all of my cousins also lived in the town. My grandma and grandpa lived there too. My cousins and I would walk the railroad tracks to a little store. We each had some money to spend. We would come out of the store with bags and bags of bubble gum, candy wax lips, cookies and cream soda. My cousins had a tent in their backyard and we would camp out at night and pig out on the treats we bought at the store. Although my life had drastically changed, I remember the times at the candy store and campouts with my cousins with happiness. I could get away from "the evil stepmother" and have some fun. When I am in a bad place in my life, I can always go back there in my mind. It always makes me feel better."

You said it well. As long as you are in charge of your thoughts, you can always find a place of solace. Looking out over a blue-green sea, noticing the flowers in the window of the local flower shop, listening to your favorite song, or remembering a campout with your cousins can indeed produce a few moments of contentment. I think you have learned your lesson well.

Congratulations,
Doc

— — —

"The memories that flow through me when I think about candy during my childhood make me smile. I remember living with my

151

grandmother in Philadelphia. We used to go to the corner store and buy red wax lips and Cabbage Patch Doll Cards with bubble gum inside. Every time I see a Push-Up Pop I remember losing my first tooth attempting to bite off a piece of it. These are all good memories for me. My grandmother was a positive influence in my life in those days. She was the only constant thing in my life after my mother died."

We certainly are resilient as children. We experience various significant negative events in our young lives and somehow we make it through them. Loving grandmothers and Cabbage Patch Doll Cards can help. Perhaps you have already been, or soon will choose to be, the "positive influence" in the life of someone close to you. It is indeed a very rewarding experience from both ends.

I wish you well,

Doc

— — —

"Yes, I remember candy dots, Tootsie Pops, and my favorite (because of the comics inside the wrapper) Bazooka Joe Bubble Gum! When I think of these childhood treats it makes me smile! I feel so happy and a little silly at the same time. I don't feel silly because I am happy, but because of all the silly things my siblings and I did for candy. Every time I enjoy some "old" candy treats it really takes me back to happier times."

I wonder if you remember licorice pipes with little red sprinkles on top of the bowl, small boxes of white candy cigarettes, penny gumball machines where a striped gumball could be exchanged for a candy bar, Turkish Taffy or BB-Bat Suckers. Those were part of my childhood, perhaps even before you were born. Ha!

I wish you special treats and happier times today.

Doc

— — —

"Here is what I believe. We, as humans and individuals, have power over our minds.

- We see what we want.
- We hear what we want.
- We feel what we want.
- We remember what we want.
- We talk about what we want and we do what we want."

You make a lot of sense. We are indeed powerful individuals with exciting potential.

Doc

— — —

"Eating a Reese's Peanut Butter Cup reminds me of when I was still in elementary school. I used to stop by my grandmother's house after school and go straight to her kitchen drawer, before I even said hello to her. She always kept the drawer stocked with Reese's for me and my sister. Whether we were there to see my grandma or scarf down her candy, she loved to see her grandchildren. Those memories have been set on the shelf but the candy reminds me they are there for our enjoyment whenever we choose."

Perhaps Grandma is still alive and you could take this opportunity to thank her for her years of love and sweet treats. And perhaps, you will have the opportunity to do the same for your grandchildren. I wish that for you.

Doc

— — —

"I would think a Tootsie Pop would only bring good memories with the good taste, but not everyone had the same childhood I did."

153

Beauty is in the eyes of the beholder, it has been said. The "goodness" or "badness" of the sucker is most certainly in the thoughts and experiences of the individual. The perception of the individual involved is the key.

Doc

"When I go back and remember the things I did when I was a child, all I can remember is the good childhood I had. My parents gave me everything, especially my mom. It is such a wonderful time to remember. I wish I could go back in time today. If I could I would be able to see my mom again. My life as a child was great. I have no complaints. If I could go back to my childhood, there is only one thing I would change. I would change many of the choices I made in my teenage years. I really should have listened to my mom!"

You remind me of the verse I learned a long time ago. "We grow too soon old and too late smart!" Often our parents were most knowledgeable about what was best for us. But the plan seems to be that we are to experiment and find out for ourselves. In fact, we could have saved ourselves a lot of bumps and bruises had we followed their instructions and wishes for us. Perhaps you will be more successful with your sons and daughters. What do you think?

I wish you lots of success and happiness with your family.

Doc

"When I remember all those fun candies when I was a child I am happy. I feel like a child again. I am happy. I feel carefree, happy and innocent. I also feel old. Not unhappy, just a little sad about the passing of time and the loss of that carefree part of my life."

I suppose there was a time when other people were responsible for us. It was a time when we depended on others for everything. Our job was to be free and do as we pleased, until we got caught. Ha! Today we are responsible for ourselves AND for others. The tables have turned. But, there ought to be times when we are carefree, happy and innocent. Isn't it possible to still have those times as adults? We can enjoy a Tootsie Pop today, for example. We can enjoy the taste TODAY without memories of the past. It simply tastes good this very moment.

I keep a box of them in my office and have for years. I enjoy one every now and then just for the shear pleasure of it. I share them with others who come to visit with me or to work with me. I am never too old for that pleasure.

I love to vacation on the Island of Eleuthera in the Bahamas. My wife and I walk the beaches there and enjoy the sand and surf every bit as much as we did as children, perhaps even more so. We feel carefree on Eleuthera and we take every chance we get to visit there. Life is short and life is to be enjoyed. I recommend YOU take time to ENJOY your life. From what I am able to understand, we only get ONE chance at life. ENJOY some moments each and everyday. Start today!

Peace,

Doc

— — —

YES I CAN!

When I was a small boy I learned something very powerful. I learned I could make my mother happy or sad, my father happy or angry, my teacher smile or frown, and my sisters pleased or upset. When I behaved as I was expected, it was reported, "David was a good boy today." When I behaved in the opposite manner, I was told that I was a bad boy. It was clear I had control over how people around me felt emotionally and my behavior equaled my worth and value as a human being.

I spent most of the next thirty years attempting to take good emotional care of myself while protecting the people around me from feeling badly. I learned that I was in charge of how other people felt, and for the most part, <u>they</u> were in charge of how I felt.

From the time I was quite young, I had friends with whom I associated on a daily basis. Some days they liked me, and some days they did not. Some days I hurt their feelings, and some days they hurt mine. It was difficult, to say the least. When I thought I had done my very best, I was told I had hurt other people's feelings, and they were sore at me. I would apologize to a friend and he might say, "I cannot get over my hurt right away! It will take some time to get over this before we can be friends again." Friendships and other relationships were, and continued to be, difficult at best. It is difficult to take care of the way another person "feels" about me.

I remember the time I met a very pretty coed during my college freshman orientation. She was a woman that I wanted to get to know better. I stopped in a candy shop in town one day and bought her a box of assorted chocolates. I had them gift-wrapped. I took the present to the women's dorm and asked my potential friend to consider going to the movies with me. I handed her the box of candy and told her I bought a present for her. She acted very pleased with my gift. She said I was sweet to have done such a nice thing for her! I knew she was happy and it was clear to me, from previous learning, that I had indeed impressed this young woman. I had made her happy!

We actually dated for a couple of months and our relationship seemed to be improving as time went on. I was pleased and she seemed to enjoy having me around. One day I remembered how well the box of chocolates had worked several months before, so I returned to the same store to purchase an identical present. I returned to my friend's dorm that night; the same young man with the same box of candy. My expectation was to be met with welcome arms. What I didn't know was that she and her roommate had just recently decided to diet to "look better for their boyfriends." This time when she saw the candy, she became instantly upset. She said I was a very inconsiderate person to give a woman candy when she was dieting! She was angry and didn't want to see me for several days.

That was a confusing and frustrating time! The first time, the candy made her happy. This time it made her upset and angry. She blamed me for her feelings on both occasions. I was most certainly responsible for how she felt. Even her roommate told me that giving her candy was an inconsiderate thing to do!

That incident was just one of the many times in my life when it was very clear I was responsible for the feelings of other people. Some people went so far as to <u>warn</u> me they "wore their feelings on their sleeves," and I "must be careful not to hurt them."

What a mess indeed! I really wasn't sure how to feel the way <u>I</u> wanted and other people were warning me to tiptoe around in <u>their</u> space so as not to upset them. It was difficult enough to take care of myself without being emotionally responsible for those around me. It appeared that I was frequently hurting someone else's feelings, or so they reported. I spent lots of time and energy being concerned and careful not to say or do things that might cause other people to blame me for their hurt feelings.

Some days I felt really good about myself for I managed to please other people. Some days the opposite was the case. My value as a human being seemed to fluctuate like the Dow Jones Average. But so be it, that's the way it was.

Several years later in college, I began to study philosophy. I was fascinated with many of the books I was reading and professors with whom I studied. One day in class, Dr. George Axtelle, the founder of the John Dewey Society, presented an interesting idea. He said that he imagined most students had been raised on the premise that, "We were bad kids if we acted badly; and we were good kids if we behaved as expected." I could easily identify with that. He went on to say that he imagined that some days we were "good" and some days we were "bad," … and some days we were "bad" in the morning and "good" by the time dad was to arrive home from work. I could also identify with that notion!

He said he had a better idea, one that would be difficult to understand and even more difficult to put into practice. He drew two circles on the board. The circle did not intersect nor did they touch one another. He made sure we saw them as completely separate. He even drew an imaginary wall between the two circles so we would know they were not related. He then explained the circle on the left is me, and the circle on the right is my behavior. He suggested that we see those two things as separate and different from one another. He said that I am not my behavior, and my behavior is not I.

Dr. Axtelle suggested that I am a valuable, fallible, human being. He said that I am a "human being" by definition, "fallible" because I am an imperfect organism that cannot avoid making mistakes and "valuable" because I am alive and have potential to do good things for the society and me. He said that I am a V.F.H.B. from birth to death, and that I cannot change. "No matter what you do, David, you will always be a valuable, fallible, human being until the day you die." He suggested that we accept this definition and move on with more important aspects of our lives.

His message became clearer as he continued to lecture to us. He was telling us to stop rating ourselves. He said the only outcome of rating ourselves was to feel badly, and healthy people do not want to make themselves feel worse than absolutely necessary.

He then moved to the second circle, which he explained contained "my behavior." He said it made sense to <u>rate behavior</u>. Sometimes we do something well and we are proud of our accomplishments. Sometimes we make a mistake and it is well to note the mistake and take corrective action. We are all fallible human beings who must error and who make lots of mistakes. It is well to note the mistakes we make and evaluate them to see if there is a better and more efficient way to behave in the future. The message was to <u>stop rating ourselves</u> and <u>only rate our behaviors</u>. It made sense, he said, to dislike some of the things we do, but it makes no sense whatsoever to dislike ourselves.

It made sense to me! As a young child in school, when I was not in my seat when the bell rang, I would be punished. I ought to be taught to respect the wishes of the teacher and be in my seat when the bell rings if that is her rule, but there is no reason to consider me a rotten kid if I am not in my seat when the bell rings. I was not a rotten kid. I was a young boy who needed to be taught to follow classroom rules. Perhaps my behavior deserves evaluation and criticism, but I do not deserve to be insulted as a whole.

Listen to the difference. First, "David, you are a rotten kid for not being in your seat when the bell rings! Can't you do what you're told and follow the rules! What's the matter with you?" Or, "David, being in your seat is important to the smooth operation of this class. I would appreciate it if you would cooperate with me and make every effort to be in your seat when the bell rings. I respect you as a member of this class, and I am asking for your cooperation."

Dr. Axtelle said that we may behave poorly or badly, but we are not poor or bad people for having done so.

In that regard, I am reminded of a woman who came to me for counseling some years later. She said, "I am unworthy of happiness in my life because I am an illegitimate person." Her mother and father were not married at the time she was conceived. She had been told several times in her life that she was illegitimate. She looked like a full-fledged human being to me. She walked and talked like a human being. She was alive and responsive as I, but <u>she</u> thought she was illegitimate. Therefore she treated herself like she was an unacceptable thing. This was even one step worse than my professor suggested. She was "bad" because her mother and father behaved "badly." She didn't even have the opportunity to earn her own badness!

I suggested that her parents' behavior did <u>not</u> make her anything other than a V.F.H.B. I also suggested that if indeed she were "illegitimate," she would not exist, and there would be nothing further to discuss. She laughed when that idea was presented to her. Her belief did not change overnight, but with help and practice she was able to accept the new notion that she <u>is</u> a legitimate, worthwhile human being who has the right and responsibility to help herself to happiness!

Food For Thought

- For whose feelings are <u>you</u> responsible?
- Who blames <u>you</u> for hurting <u>their</u> feelings? How do they say you do it?
- What do you think differently now that you have read this story?
- Are you considering rating <u>only</u> your <u>behavior</u>, and <u>not</u> your <u>value</u> as a human being? Would that be a significant change for you?
- You are a V.F.H.B!

ANALYSIS OF ATTITUDES

"Since reading this story, I pay attention to how I react to other people's moods. If I start to get angry or my feelings start to get hurt, I say to myself, "You do not have to bother yourself about this." And, it is working! It's not 100%, but I am way more in control of my

feelings. Other people's comments don't affect me nearly as much as they used to."

We really are powerful creatures who have enormous control over ourselves. It is fun to understand that we DO have control over our thoughts, feelings and physical behaviors. We do not have to suffer at the hands of others. Congratulations on your new insights. Keep on reading, thinking and writing. It makes a powerful difference in your life and mine.

Doc

— — —

"Sometimes my family blames me for their feelings. It seems impossible to please my family all the time. I have such difficulty doing everything they expect of me."

No kidding! Pleasing others can often be an impossible task, especially when their expectations are not in line with what you want. Other people want you to behave as they want, and you behave as you want. Therein lies the conflict. When you don't do what I want, I am disappointed. That does not mean you have done something wrong, it just means that you didn't do what I wanted or expected.

When I came out of my mother, the doctor cut my umbilical cord which separated me from her. It also made me my own person. It meant that soon, I was going to be free to be me, and free to make my own choices in my life. It also meant that, someday soon, I was going to be able to behave as I want. Others have the same wonderful opportunity.

Moms and Dads are wise to realize that their children have minds of their own. They are the captains of their own ships just as the parents are. Children march to their own drummers and make their own decisions. Once, in a wonderful professional workshop, I was told that I don't own my children. My children are not "mine." I did help bring them into this world, but they do not belong to me. They are not my property and at least by the age of maturity I ought to realize that they are responsible for their lives, not I.

Often my sons behave as they want, not as I want. I clearly recognize their behavior as <u>their</u> choice, not mine. I don't have to like their behavior, but I also don't have to upset myself when they behave as they have the right to behave. They are their own individual persons. I am not in control or their behavior, and don't really want to be. I am certainly not the source of all wisdom.

It is not my responsibility to please other people. It is my responsibility to live my life as I see fit. It is not your responsibility to please your family. It is their responsibility to please themselves.

From what I have seen, you are making many positive efforts to build a quality life for yourself. Be proud of what you see in your bathroom mirror. Do what you think best for you. I have enjoyed watching your academic progress this year!

Doc

– – –

"Sometimes I really waste too much time and energy trying to please others and forgetting about taking really good care of myself and what my goals are."

It is indeed very important to value yourself. You are the most important person in your life and I would suggest that you take very good care of you. I think your statement is accurate and I appreciate your insight.

Doc

– – –

"Having had two abusive relationships, one with my mother and the other with my ex-husband, I have been down the path of feeling worthless. I thought I was responsible for making them angry and I was responsible for their abuses of me. Now I know differently. My challenge now is my children. I set a positive example for them. I cannot control their thoughts and actions. I have tried to teach them that they do not have to be miserable and unhappy. After reading,

"Yes I Can," I realize that I am leaving out an important part of their education. They are responsible for their own feelings and happiness. Half of my life I have spent being an unhealthy human being. I want my children to be healthy."

I am continually amazed at how much responsibility we are willing to assume for other people's feelings. For example, if you don't like me, do you have the right to abuse me? Not so!

Some people are sick-in-the-head. Some people hate or dislike themselves. They treat themselves, as well as the people around them, with hatred, dislike, disrespect and abuse. It is possible to assume that because they treat you badly, you must be bad. Just because you believe it does not make it true. Being treated badly is not evidence you are bad! It usually means the person who is treating you badly is unhappy, miserable, or just plain goofy. It does not mean it is time to dislike your self. But, often that is hard to understand.

The excitement for you is that you seem to clearly understand it now. You do not deserve abuse!

Continue to remind your children that they were not the cause of the abuse they experienced. Remind them also that their mother did not deserve the abuse she received. Tell them time and time again, they are beautiful children who do not deserve to be abused, ever!

You are on the right track. Continue to take care of each other. Continue to value yourself and your children. I wish you happiness.

Doc

$$- - -$$

"I am responsible for my wife's feelings, according to her. She says that whenever I do not compliment what she is wearing, or tease her, it upsets her. I am not trying to upset her, and when I tease her, I immediately tell her I am joking, but it does not seem to matter at that point. She is still upset. After reading this story I realize I should not tease her as much. I should take her feelings and wishes into account. She is the love of my life, and the one I will spend the rest of my life with. I am going to stop teasing her as much and start giving her more compliments."

You know what you do to give your wife reason to be upset. You tease her. You say she is the "love of your life," and you want to spend the rest of your life with her. It would seem that if you want to spend the rest of your life with her, you would stop teasing her altogether. Teasing gives her reason to be upset with you. There is <u>no</u> need to tease someone you love and someone you want to be around you forever. STOP acting in ways that you know are upsetting to your best friend!

Your wife seems to ENJOY compliments. Compliments feel good to most people. If you want your bride to spend the rest of her life with you, COMPLIMENT HER. It takes very little energy on your part and it feels a hell of a lot better than teasing.

Getting along well as married partners is not rocket science. You know that she likes some of your behaviors. Repeat those often. You know she does not like others. Refrain from repeating those.

Do not be less annoying. Simply STOP annoying her. She'll likely stick around longer.

I wish you both well, indeed.

Doc

— — —

"My children blame me for their hurt feelings. They probably think that way because I blame them for my hurt feelings. After reading this story, it seems that blaming others for my hurt feelings is more like a guilt trip. I feel bad so I want you to feel bad also. Then we'll both feel bad and I'll feel better knowing you feel bad. It seems so silly to think that I behave this way everyday. I should say, "I expected you to do something for me and you didn't. Let's figure this out together. Then no one needs to feel badly, including me."

I imagine your children behave in ways other than the ways you want and expect. When you don't get what you want from them, <u>you</u> upset yourself. "I can't have what I want from my kids so I will also upset myself." Not getting everything you want from your children does not require you to feel badly. No parent gets everything they want from their children. "Oh well, they are just children and will never act exactly like I want them to act." And, *when life does not treat me as I very much want it to, I can decide what to think, and therefore, how to feel.* I am an adult and know that I cannot have everything in life the way I would prefer it to be. I am really only in charge of me.

Perhaps you ought to take some time, once a week, and talk to your children about <u>who</u> and <u>what</u> controls the way they think and feel. It would be good practice for you and a wonderful, new education for your children. You would each get better at being individually responsible for your feelings.

It sounds like an exciting idea to me. How about you?

Doc

— — —

"My son's father used to make me feel terrible. He had a serious drug problem and he would accuse me of all sorts of things. He would often be angry and yell at me. When I left him because of his habit he told me I broke his heart and he wanted to die. It hurt me badly to hurt someone else. After reading this story it is comforting to know that it was not my fault his feelings were hurt when I left him. I do not believe I am a bad person and neither is he, despite the bad things he did."

Your note to me reminds me of when I lived in Indiana. I was the only psychologist in several small towns that our mental health centers served. Soon after arriving in Indiana, the Sheriff would get me out of bed around 2:00 a.m. on Sunday morning to counsel the drunks that he had arrested after the bars closed. I had to laugh at this behavior. I asked the Sheriff why he didn't talk to the men and women himself. He said, "They're drunk and they make no sense. I thought with <u>your</u> skills, you could make sense out of their conversations." I explained that a drugged mind did and said things that were hard-to-impossible to understand. What made the most sense was to <u>wait</u> until the folks were sober and then talk with them.

I've spent more than 15 years counseling with drug-abusers. It is difficult work. The habituated or addicted bodies want drugs and will say and do just about anything to get them. They will lie, cheat, steal and prostitute to feed their habits. They will indeed do their best to make <u>others</u> feel guilt for <u>their</u> drug habits. Only <u>once</u> have I met a drug-abuser who could honestly say that someone else was responsible for their drug habit. But, the abuser wants you to believe you have some responsibility for their habit. It just isn't the case.

I would imagine you did the rational thing when you made the decision to get out of the relationship. Someone needs to survive the craziness! In your case, <u>you</u> survived.

You <u>didn't</u> "break his heart." You <u>didn't</u> "hurt him." You <u>didn't</u> hurt his feelings when you divorced him.

I agree with you, he isn't a bad person. On the other hand, his <u>behavior</u> was intolerable and you did not have to put up with it. You also did not have to put up with his abuse of you.

It appears to me you made a rational, in your own best interest, decision.

I recommend you continue to take very good care of <u>you</u>.

Doc

— — —

"After I read this story I realized that although I am not perfect, I am still a good person. I also think I could be more considerate of others."

The fact is you could not attain perfection if you tried. You'd probably only drive yourself crazy in the process. Imperfection comes with being human. We are mistake-making creatures. It's just the way we are.

And yes, you are indeed a good person. If the only good to come from writing these stories is that <u>you</u> discovered your goodness, then my efforts have not been in vain. I can rest easy tonight. Thanks!

Being "considerate of others" is a loving virtue. It is one that makes the world a better place in which to live. I encourage you to be more considerate of others, yes indeed.

And, thanks for sharing.

Doc

— — —

CHAD CANNOT BE ROTTEN

- A Children's Story (Or, is it?) -

Not long ago, Chad and his brother, and his Mom and Dad, moved to a new house. The new house was in a new town, a long, long, way from their old house.

Chad liked his old house, and his old school, and friends. He had no idea at all what the new house would be like. He'd rather not move but the whole family was moving, and he didn't want to stay at the old house by himself.

His Dad was happy going to a new job, his Mother was happy going to a new house, and his brother was happy because he would have his own bedroom.

Chad decided to be happy too.

When he saw the new house he liked it. Chad liked the big yard, and the cornfield across the road. He liked the rickety wooden bridge across the creek, just down the road from his new home. He liked the whole world.

When Chad's Mom enrolled him at Hilltop School he went gladly, and he liked it. He met some new kids, and he thought they were "super".

The world was just the way it should be. When he went to sleep at night he just scrunched right down into the pillow. He liked to fall asleep fast and dream about building a dam across the creek.

In the morning, he liked to think about all the good stuff he would do during the day.

During the second week of school, his teacher explained a kind of game they were going to play. There was a big red apple hung on the bulletin board for each pupil in the class. If a pupil misbehaved, the teacher would put a little brown worm on the apple. If the apple accumulated five worms it would be called a rotten apple and fall to the ground. The rotten apple student would get a spanking in front of the class.

None of this made too much of an impression on Chad. Nobody was going to misbehave! And nobody would get spanked in school! It was just one of those things that grown-ups talk about.

One day while Miss Miller was out of the classroom one of the boys stood up and whispered real loud, "Miss Miller is a diller". Chad didn't think that made any sense, but everyone laughed when they heard it. So, he stood up and said, "Miss Miller is a diller". The unfortunate thing was that Miss Miller walked into the classroom just as he said it!

She was upset. She definitely believed that little boys should not poke fun at their teachers. Chad could tell by looking at her face that she was displeased. He wished he hadn't stood up and said, "Miss Miller is a diller".

"Chad", said Miss Miller, "I can tell that you want a rotten apple. You certainly earned a worm by being bad today!" With that she took a brown worm out of her desk and pasted it on the apple with Chad's name on it.

Some of the children laughed when they saw this. Chad laughed too, to show that he wasn't worried - but he was worried. He didn't know how he had gotten into such a predicament.

He liked Miss Miller. He liked her from the very first time he saw her. Now she had put a worm on his apple and he thought that they weren't friends any more. He wished he could go home. He wished he didn't have to stay in school. He didn't like having a rotten apple.

At recess he didn't feel like playing catch with his friends. He sat and watched. They seemed to be having a good time without him. He thought how lucky those kids were, not having worms on their apples as he did.

From that day on, Chad was very, very, careful not to do anything that Miss Miller might get upset about. He certainly did not want another worm on his apple. School wasn't fun anymore. It was mostly trying to stay out of trouble.

While Chad worried about staying out of trouble, and worried about getting another worm, other children were not so lucky. John Slocum got in trouble every day. By the middle of the second week he had five worms on his apple. The teacher let the rotten apple fall off the bulletin board and land on the floor. Then John Slocum had to come to the front of the room and Miss Miller gave him a spanking.

Chad was horrified.

John Slocum shed a few tears.

Chad dreamed about a rotten apple that night. He tried to pin it back on the bulletin board but it kept falling off.

The next morning Chad did not want to go to school. He didn't want to even look at his apple with the worm on it. When his mother asked him why he didn't want to go to school he said it was because he felt rotten.

Chad's mother decided that he wasn't sick and that he should go to school.

The children were surprised to find that all of the apples had been taken down from the bulletin board! One of the little girls whose apple didn't have any worms on it asked Miss Miller where the apples were. Miss Miller replied, "I don't know what I have to do to get you children to behave, but the apples did not work, so I will have to think of something else."

Chad was delighted.

John Slocum hollered, "HOORAY!" real loud, and Miss Miller looked very stern.

It wasn't long before Miss Miller did think of something else. The fact that Thanksgiving was approaching gave her the idea. She pasted pretty pumpkin faces all around the room, one for each pupil. Chad's name was on one of the pumpkins. Chad smiled a big smile. His pumpkin smiled a big smile back. Chad felt comfortable. Every-time he looked at his pumpkin it was looking right back at him.

At recess, John Slocum was over by the book cabinet and Miss Miller told him to take his seat. He didn't hear her. Miss Miller told him a second time to take his seat. He heard her that time and said, "Okay, Miss Miller," but stayed at the book cabinet to finish whatever it was he was doing.

Miss Miller went over to John's pumpkin and plucked off one of its eyebrows. "You can just take home a horrible looking pumpkin at Thanksgiving because you are a horrible boy," said Miss Miller. "How can I get this class to behave if no one will listen!" she complained.

Poor John Slocum watched his pumpkin disappear during the next two weeks. Once he pushed a girl, not purposely of course, and he had trouble with talking when Miss Miller wanted to talk. All the while Poor Chad thought continuously about how he wanted to escape having his pumpkin destroyed.

Now, he didn't want to go to school, and was usually sick when it was time to go. He especially liked Saturdays, Sundays, and days when there were teacher's meetings. He was now uncomfortable in school with his pumpkin looking down at him.

Miss Miller told Chad that she wished he would talk a little louder when she spoke to him. He always answered her very, very, quietly, and most of the time he sort of turned his head sideways so he could have his pumpkin in sight. So Miss Miller had trouble hearing him when he answered in class. But, he didn't want his pumpkin to look rotten, with maybe a missing nose or eyebrow. He even sat down quietly, not banging his seat like some other kids.

Chad never worried too much about what Miss Miller was teaching. He figured <u>that</u> was far less important than protecting his pumpkin which, thank goodness, was still whole.

Miss Miller decided that Chad was just a daydreamer, and his report card was marked to show that he did not pay attention.

Chad's Mom and Dad talked to him about his report card, and his reluctance to go to school and his lack of interest in school activities. Then they talked to some of the other parents. The pupils did not want to be rotten in school and bring home rotten pumpkins to their parents!

Getting a rotten pumpkin and having the other kids call you rotten was no fun at all!

The children in Miss Miller's class were very much surprised to come to school one day and find that all the pumpkins had been taken down and were nowhere to be found. They asked Miss Miller about the missing pumpkins. She said that she had taken them down and that the pupils were not to concern themselves with <u>why</u> they were down. Chad didn't know what was wrong, but he knew <u>something</u> was wrong. He wished that he lived in Willie Wonka's Chocolate Factory.

When the first snow fell, Miss Miller gave the children some construction paper and they each made a snowman to hang on the classroom wall. When Chad made the mouth on his snowman he made it straight across, and the snowman looked rather sad that way. Chad wished he had made the mouth curved up so that the snowman would look smiley.

Even after the snowmen were hung, Chad wished he had made the mouth smiley. He asked Miss Miller if he could make the snowman's head over again. Miss Miller said he shouldn't bother because by the time Christmas came most of the snowmen wouldn't have hats, or heads, or arms, because of the rotten children and the rotten way they behaved in class.

I'm going to take home a rotten snowman home at Christmas time, thought Chad. He looked at the snowman, and it looked sadder than when he made it. Instead of the mouth being straight across it seemed to droop a little bit at the corners!

On Saturday morning, Chad's father asked him why he was moping around instead of going out to play with his best friend. "I feel rotten," Chad said, because by Christmas time my snowman will be rotten and I won't want to bring it home."

"Chad," said his father, "I love you, and your happiness is important to me. I want you to come outside by the basketball hoop for a minute." Chad went out with his father. His father tossed the basketball to Chad and said, "Let's see you make ten baskets in a row." Chad laughed and said, "I can't do that, you know. I'm not a champ basketball player." He tossed the ball, and missed, and tried again, and missed, and then the third time he made a basket. His father said, "Now you see son, you missed the basket a couple of times, but that does not mean you are a rotten person."

"I would like for you to behave as intelligently as you can, be as wise as you know how, and just do your best at school and at play. There is no sense trying to figure out who is the rottenest kid in your class."

"You can easily figure out who plays ball the best, or who spells the best, or who has the biggest feet. There is nothing wrong with that."

"But picking the rottenest kid is **NOT** in your best interest. There is **NO SUCH THING** as a rotten person."

"There may be rotten apples, but **NOT** rotten human beings! Instead of worrying, it would be so much better if you would just quit measuring who is rottenest and simply go to school and know that you are Chad. Just be Chad!"

"If you have a spelling bee and don't do well in it, you can tell yourself that you didn't spell well. You won't have to worry about being a rotten person, you can just choose to study spelling a little bit more."

"If people tell you that you are rotten, you will know better than to believe them because you and I know that **YOU CANNOT BE ROTTEN**, no matter what. The same thing applies if they tell you that you are bad or horrible. It is just not true!"

"You will always be Chad, no matter how you behave!"

Chad **CANNOT** Be Rotten! And, neither can you!

Food For Thought

- Have you ever felt rotten, or thought you were risking becoming rotten because of something you did? What were the circumstances?
- Was it you who was being critical of your behavior, or was it someone else? What was being said about you?
- How would you handle the situation today? How would your thinking change today? Please be specific with your response.

ANALYSIS OF ATTITUDES

"When I look in the mirror, I always find something wrong with me. I find everyone else better than me."

I remember taking a spelling quiz on a Friday in the 3rd grade and earning a 9 out of 10 points. The comment from the teacher was, "Why did you miss one?" Then a comment from a friend or a parent was, "Why did you miss that one? Next time, get them all right!" It was the one that I missed that seemed to get the attention. It was what I did wrong that was noticed.

Our grading system in the schools is negative also. In the public schools and in the colleges, 59% is an "F." If I score 59, out of 100, on a test, I have "failed." And yet, 59% means that I answered "more than half correctly." I answered the <u>majority</u> of the questions correctly. So where is my "failure"?

I remember asking one of my students, who was critical of the way she looked, to <u>imagine</u> she was looking into the mirror and seeing the face of her <u>daughter</u>. What would she see? She said she loved her daughter and thought she was very pretty. She would not notice the freckles or the eyebrow out of place, or even her nose that was not perfectly straight. She would indeed tell her daughter, "You are the prettiest girl in the world!" But, seeing <u>herself</u> in the mirror, she would not be that kind.

It is a critical and often cruel world. We tend to notice the imperfections in others as they tend to do with us. We seem to find fault more commonly than we offer praise. We have spent years practicing and learning the habit of critical self-negativity.

You and I do not deserve to be insulted. We deserve to be liked, loved and respected, especially from within.

Psychological studies indicate that we generally have lower self-esteem than we deserve. Indeed folks have been suggesting for years that we ought to think better of ourselves. We have learned the habit of negative self-esteem. We accept the negative feedback of others. We look in the mirror and dislike what we see, because others have been critical of us. We take others' opinions seriously and adopt a negative self-image. We come to believe what others say about us and pretend it is reality.

You are unhappy with your looks. "I look in the mirror and always find something wrong with me!" But indeed, you don't like that attitude. You don't like looking in your mirror and seeing something less than suitable. You want to appear more satisfactory to yourself. You want to look in the mirror and think, "I look great! I am great!" The good news is you have that choice! In fact, you have lots of choices.

You need a new attitude. You could benefit from a new script. Did you know that, "You are in charge of what you THINK?" And, that includes how you THINK you LOOK! Do you know that merely thinking you look good, effects the way others think you look?

Try this. Look in your mirror and say, *"Wow, what a great looking gal! I like what I see! If the image in the mirror was that of my daughter, I would be proud and happy. I am proud of me, and happy that I look as good as I do. I accept myself as I am. I like myself as I am. I can even love myself as I am."*

My self-concept is <u>mine</u>. I create it, I make it up, and it will be mine as long as I live. I can accept my image of myself as it presently is, or I can create a new one. It is up to me to decide what I would <u>like to think of myself</u>. I will <u>write down how I would like to think</u>. The final step is to <u>practice my new thinking until it becomes my new attitude</u>.

The part I like most is that my self-concept is truly mine. I have the choice of changing it anytime I want to accept the responsibility and spend time practicing a new way of thinking. That's exciting, don't you agree? Our self-concepts are not "set in stone." They belong to us as individuals. We can do with them as we please.

So start today. Stand in front of your mirror and talk to yourself as though you were someone special (because you are). See yourself for your good qualities. For the moment, <u>ignore</u> the flaws. Highlight your strengths. Praise yourself. Smile back at the mirror image. Laugh out-loud, if it will help. You might even think how silly it <u>was</u> to see such a pretty, warm, caring, and loving person as yourself in a negative light.

"It is <u>time</u> to care for me in a more loving and respectful manner! Why? I deserve to be treated with love and respect, especially by myself!"

Start now!

Doc

— — —

"Often in the morning, when I wake up, I am in a bad mood. I say to myself, 'I'm in a bad mood and I can't change it, even if I want to. I think I have little control over me.'"

First, you have control of your behavior (thoughts, emotions and physical behavior)!

Perhaps it will help to tell you a true story of a favorite patient of mine. Her name was Louise, and she lived in Indiana. Louise spent most of her life helping handicapped children. She worked hard and long to do whatever was necessary to make their lives better. She was known throughout the county as a loving, caring and dedicated teacher. Her energy was boundless and she was available to her students and their families whenever they felt they needed her. She loved her students and she loved making their lives more useful and enjoyable. Some called her a living angel.

Louise spent more than 40 years teaching. One day it was time to retire. She was tired and deserved a rest. She left teaching and went home to relax. Soon she was miserable. She missed the students and families that once meant so very much to her. Her life, she said, felt empty and without purpose now. She was sad and referred to herself as "depressed."

Louise came to ask for my help. She said that her life seemed not worth living. She didn't like the way she felt.

As we talked, I had an idea. I asked Louise, "What is the first thing you think, or the first thing you say to yourself in the morning when you awaken to the sound of your alarm?" Without hesitation, Louise said, "Oh shit, another day!"

Understand? My day, your day, and Louise's day would have to start out poorly were we to awaken with the very same thought. That seems very clear. If we want to have a positive start to our day, we need a positive attitude. Where does the positive attitude come from? It comes from within us. How does it get there? We have to insist it be there!

Would you like a suggestion? End your day with something positive to say about the day you just completed. Write down your thoughts in a paragraph or two. "Today I am especially pleased that I was able to help my neighbor who is ill and would have had nothing good to eat had I not made dinner and taken it to her." Read your thoughts once more and feel good about what you accomplished today. Now, make a conscious effort to think of something worthwhile to do tomorrow ... a reason to wake up feeling positive. "Tomorrow I am going to get all my washing and ironing done. That chore will then be behind me and I will be pleased with myself for that accomplishment." At the end of the day tomorrow, record that you made some positive progress and feel good about having done so. "Gee, it feels good to have a closet of clean clothes once again! That was another task well done!" Then record another reason to wake up tomorrow with positive goals. "Tomorrow I am going to attend class as scheduled, and will look for ten new things I've learned in class. I will attend class with a positive attitude. I am a college student and I am realizing a personal dream."

I bet you have a positive sense of accomplishment just reading the above thoughts. If you look for something positive to accomplish, and something positive to think while achieving your goal, you are most likely to be thinking and feeling positive. That's your goal: positive thoughts AND positive feelings about your life.

You will be in a good mood, and you will have increased your sense of self-control.

Congratulations to you!!

Doc

— — —

"I have a habit of telling the people I love what to do all the time. I can't control it... it's a force of habit."

Ah yes, the old "force of habit" behavior, also known as, "I have always done it that way," and "I was born that way and it's who I am!"

Well, I am here to tell you your behavior is not genetically determined (you weren't born that way), and you have not <u>always</u> done it that way. Your desire to control the behavior of the people around you is <u>learned</u>. You weren't pushy when you were born. You learned to be that way, long after birth. The exciting news is that, because your behavior is <u>learned</u>, you can change your mind, adopt a new attitude, and act <u>differently</u>. I enjoy saying, "I am trainable." You are trainable also.

The fact is that *people do what they want, not what you and I want!* You and I have enough difficulty controlling our own behavior (thoughts, feelings & actions) without pretending we have control of other peoples' behavior. You may <u>want</u> to control others, but you really cannot.

Besides, you, like the rest of us, are simply a fallible human being who makes mistakes, lots of them. You cannot act <u>perfectly</u> and understand everything. Neither can I. You are not my boss, and I am not yours. You don't have to march to my drummer, and I can choose not to march to yours. You didn't come into this world to rule me, and I am not in charge of you.

There are people who think <u>they</u> are the <u>best</u> driver on the road. Others think that they know <u>best</u> how to raise children. Still more believe that their Lexus makes them <u>better</u> humans; others with little polo players on their shirts believe they are going to heaven and you're not; and still others who were born on the "better side" of the tracks turn up their noses at you and me. Their thinking does not make it so.

Why not lead your life, as best you can, and allow me to do the same? Why not see how educated and wise <u>you</u> can become while not attempting to run my life for me, unless of course, I ask for your help. Give up taking responsibility for the lives of the people around you. You will be freer to do a better job with yourself.

I like being me. I respect you, being you. I am more than willing to let you make choices in life and become the person you would like to become. I would like the same respect from you. Your parents' love and approval is not a prerequisite for your personal happiness. Your family can behave as <u>they</u> want, not as you want, and you can be a happy, well-adjusted person.

<u>Stop</u> bossing other people around. It's a nuisance, and they will like you more when you <u>do</u> stop!!!

Doc

— — —

"Hi, Professor! I drink way too much Pepsi! I drink it without thinking. Can you please do something to help me?"

Perhaps it's <u>time</u> to <u>start thinking</u> about it! You already have, because you wrote to me with your concern.

Research the problem. Have you any idea what is in a can of Pepsi? Lots of sugar, that's for sure. Our psychology text says that soft drinks contain approximately a dozen, or more, teaspoons of sugar! How does that sound? If you ordered a glass of iced tea in a restaurant, would you add 12 teaspoons of sugar to it? I don't believe so.

What about the caffeine in the drinks. How much does each can contain? Is caffeine good for your body? Do you care?

If you "drink too much Pepsi" then it must be your habit has taken over and you are a "Puppet." Have you read my story entitled, <u>Puppets</u>? I suggest you do as soon as possible. It is likely to help change your Pepsi-habit.

In the meantime, remember <u>you</u> control what you drink! The "drink" is not in charge, nor is "it" responsible for your behavior. You may indeed have a "Pepsi-drinking-habit," but that habit <u>is</u> under <u>your</u> control.

Doc

— — —

"Dr. Brown, the habit I would like to eliminate completely is my smoking habit. I choose to ignore the fact that I would like to quit smoking. Smoking has made a puppet of me!"

Hmmmmmmmmmm! You must choose! You must choose to (1) "eliminate my smoking habit completely," <u>or</u> (2) "choose to ignore that fact." There is a little humor in your comment. You would like to achieve your goal, <u>but</u> you choose to ignore it. So, what's it going to be?

You may be an addict. You are most likely addicted to cigarettes. Maybe we should be kinder and refer to you as a "druggie?" Nicotine is a drug. You could admit yourself to a drug rehabilitation unit in a local hospital, or admit yourself to the addictions' unit of a mental health center. You could throw away all the little cylinders stuffed with dead leaves and STOP smoking today.

You control what you put in your mouth! You didn't smoke when you were born. You learned that stinking habit later in life. Perhaps you wanted to "look mature," and started smoking like some older kids you knew. Or, you wanted women to like you and believed that women liked men who smoke. Or, did you learn to believe, "Salem Cigarettes are indeed a breath of springtime," and rather than go on expensive vacations to Switzerland you stayed home and smoked instead.

If you were like me, you learned to smoke because the manufacturers passed out free samples on the street corners where you lived. They knew the drugs in their dead leaves, as well as the drugs they added to the dead leaves, would soon help us have a new habit ... smoking!

It's popular to have difficulty getting rid of the habit. Lots of folks will tell you, "It is impossible to quit, I've tried and failed, and tried, and failed!" There are pills, patches, chewing gum, hypnosis, books, tapes, shrinks, and more.

What you really need is to make a determined, conscious decision, **"This is my last cigarette!"** Tell everyone you know, "I have stopped smoking! I am now free and clear of the habit!" Never put one in your mouth ever again. Can you do it? Of course you can!!!! Whether or not you will is another question. It is probably easier not to quit. Later in life, you can simply blame the cigarette companies for "making you smoke." But then, your consequence will likely be poor health, or death. But, who cares, right? "We all have to die of something!"

Come on. Love yourself! Respect yourself! Research says that smoking is highly correlated with low self-esteem. You deserve better! Besides, you are going to smell better as a non-smoker. Throw away your cancer sticks and join the proud group of people who like themselves enough to NOT smoke.

You <u>can</u> quit. Be a quitter, and live!

Doc

— — —

"I have been smoking for 19 years and recently quit for seven months. For some unknown reason, I started back at it again one day when I was mad. I cannot get myself to stop again."

I wonder why it is when we get down on ourselves, we seem to punish ourselves even more than we deserve.

You stopped smoking. You got angry, and some of that anger was most likely directed at yourself. So, what the heck, as long as you are in this mess, you might as well start smoking again too. Or, you used to smoke when you were angry to "ease your tensions?" Or, when you are angry, you think you look "cool" when you smoke? Or, you look "mean" when you smoke. It is hard to read your mind from this distance. I am not convinced that the "reasons" why you started smoking again really matter anyway.

Think about this. You quit for seven months. That means that you can quit for <u>another</u> 7 months. That would be a heck of a lot better than continuing to smoke! Right?

How did you talk yourself into quitting last time? Those reasons are still valid today. Think about the last time you quit. Quit again, now!

Perhaps you "cannot" stop again because you don't deserve to stop. Perhaps you did something that you are unwilling to forgive yourself for. Forgive yourself for the cause of your anger and move on. Once again decide that you are worth not abusing yourself with tobacco.

You are a <u>fallible </u>human being. You are less than perfect; never to attain perfection in your lifetime. You are a mistake-making individual; just like the rest of us. I am sure that some of your anger is directed at yourself. You err and then you dislike yourself for your errors. Dislike the <u>behavior</u> and leave yourself alone! We all do damn, dumb things. We are all human. Learn from your errors and move on. Spend as little time punishing yourself for your mistakes as you can. Learn not to make the same mistake again, if it is possible. That's the goal.

You're in college now. You are learning to have more control over your life and you are learning to change some of your habits. You have lots of options and choices. Choose to quit smoking. If you relapse, quit smoking again. I trust that eventually you will get it right.

I have faith in you!

Doc

– – –

"Since I was 12 years old I bite my fingernails. I do not have control over this behavior at all."

I think you are right! You must have eaten something you weren't supposed to eat at age 12 and it caused you to bite your fingernails for the rest of your life. Or, you were frightened by a giant gator and the gator forced you to bite your nails. Or, "the devil made you do it!" For sure, you are out of control! There is no hope for you for the rest of your days on this earth. Bite, bite, and bite. You are doomed! You will have to bite and bite until your nails are gone and then you will start to eat your fingers!!!

Does this begin to sound pretty silly to you? I hope so. You were not born biting your nails. You started when you were 12. Now that you are 23, you can STOP the habit.

I want to share the "A,B,C's of Becoming a Non-Fingernail-Biter" with you. Here they are. Put these to use and join the majority of people your age. (A) Imagine yourself as a non-biter. How does it feel to see you as someone who does not bite her nails? Great feeling, right?! Now, decide that you have the control. Say, "I am in control of what I put in my mouth! I am not going to bite my fingernails anymore. I have begun a new habit of growing pretty fingernails!" There! You now have the beginning of a new habit. (B) At bedtime, remind yourself that you are a non-fingernail biter. Write the statement on a pad of paper and leave it on the night stand next to your bed. Read that note each morning when you wake up. "I am in control of what I put in my mouth! I am not going to bite my fingernails anymore. I have begun a new habit of growing pretty fingernails!" (C) Carry the note with you and read it 6 times each day. Read the note 6 times today, and again when you go to bed tonight. Tomorrow, and for the next 7 days, repeat this process.

You will be proud to realize that you are now in control of what you put in your mouth, and you won't bite your fingernails anymore.

Congratulations!

Doc Brown (-:/

— — —

"My excessive late night snacking is one habit I would like to eliminate. I started this behavior after I ended my relationship with my fiancé. I was sad and depressed."

Food has long been used as a form of "self-medication." We enjoy eating. For most of us it is a pleasurable experience. If I am feeling sad, a nice piece of chocolate cake with a scoop of chocolate chip ice cream can make my life seem a little brighter. It is no secret, we eat to live, and we also eat for pleasure.

So your fiancé left. You were feeling sad and rejected, and you used food to make yourself feel better and ease the pain. Not hard to understand, and very common indeed. You are not alone in that regard.

You are smart enough to know when your habit started and why. You are intelligent enough, therefore, to change your behavior. You didn't have your "excessive late night snacking" before you met your fiancé, and you don't need it now. You are in control of your eating. You can decide you don't need the "late night snacking" anymore.

Make a conscious decision that tonight you are going to bed without "excessive snacking." If you would like a snack before bed, decide during the day what it will be. Lay out your bedtime snack long before bed. You can look forward to having a snack, and you will have planned what the snack will be. It will be reasonable and not excessive.

Once you have made it through your first night, you can take pride in the fact that you are in control and the excess at bedtime has come to an end.

Remember, decide during the day what is reasonable to have as a bedtime snack. Define the snack and the portion. Imagine yourself

183

feeling <u>comfortable</u> enjoying the snack that you are making for yourself. Imagine it being <u>enough</u> to satisfy you.

In the evening, treat yourself to that snack, while telling yourself that you are overcoming the habit! "I am sure proud of me for taking charge of my life! I don't need my old fiancé, and I don't need food for medication. I have my present life to enjoy. I am proud of my progress! Congratulations to me!!!" Doc

– – –

"I would like to be more useful at home. I tend to come home from work or school and watch TV or go to bed. I want to try to learn to be more productive with my extra time."

I want to be completely frank with you. The truth is that your <u>wife</u> wants you "to be more useful at home," not you. Am I correct? If <u>you</u> wanted to be more useful at home, you would be. There is no one standing in your way. My supposition is that you could help with the washing and ironing anytime you want, and it would be appreciated. Your wife will not argue, "Hey, stop that! It's my job!" On the contrary, you will get a gold star next to your name the day you choose to help.

I will bet if you got home from school before your wife, and you prepared dinner for the two of you, she would love the surprise. She would not argue and say, "That was my job and I wish you would let me do all the housework!" Would she?

If you wash the dishes after dinner rather than watching television, will she complain? I doubt it. If you wash the kitchen floor so she does not have to spend Saturday morning doing it, she will appreciate the kindness.

Buy an appointment book. Cross out time for work, for school, and for study. Make time for meals, exercise, dates with your wife and mowing the grass. Find time for household chores and pencil them in also. You could start with two a week. Decide on two ways to be "more useful at home." You might even ask your wife for some specific suggestions; I imagine she has some to recommend. Schedule your time to be able to complete the two chores. Then, "Git er done!"

You are a full-time student and you have a job. You are a busy man; there is no doubt about it. Your wife works full-time and also attends class. She is a busy person too. You two also have a home to run. That's no small task either. But it is <u>manageable</u>. Millions of people before you have done all three, and have done them well. A schedule can make a significant difference in your life. Start by working on your schedule everyday. You could substitute 1 hour per day of TV with music and that will be your work time.

You're a good student. I trust that you can achieve your goal with a little more effort on your part. I believe that (1) making a daily schedule will really help you find some "free-time," and (2) turning off the television will be just as helpful.

My favorite philosophy professor, Dr. George Axtelle, once said, "No one has ever drowned in their own sweat!"

I wish you well!

Doc

— — —

"I would like to stop doubting myself. I'm constantly telling myself, "I can't do it!"

Yes indeed! If I constantly tell myself I can't do something, then I will eventually believe it.

On the very first day my freshman classes begin, during the first ten minutes, I tell the students, "This course is <u>doable</u>!" Do you know why I do that? On the very first day of school for my sons, I told them time and time again, "You are going to <u>love school</u>. You are going to have a <u>great teacher</u> and you are going to <u>love learning</u>!" Why would I say that? While my sons were growing up, I told each of them thousands of times, "You are bright young men. You <u>can</u> do it!" Do you know why I said that?

There is nothing like <u>positive</u> feedback, and there is nothing like <u>positive</u> self-talk to help make a person powerful, capable and productive.

Start by saying, **"I CAN! I WILL! I CAN!!"** That's the 1st step. Each and every time, "I can't," pops into your head, follow it with an

185

enthusiastic, **"OH YES, I CAN!"** Attitudes do not die easily, so you need to be enthusiastic and stubborn about getting rid of the old one.

I think you ought to stand in front of your mirror, and just as a great actress might say her lines, you say, **"I am a woman of great potential! I have many things in my life that I am proud of, and I have many more to accomplish. I have strengths, talents and potential. I am a positive and creative human being. I can do many things, and I <u>can</u> do them well!"**

You see, the difference between "I can't" and "I can" is the modification of one word. The exciting thing is that one word makes all the difference in the world. You might even do as I have suggested to others, write the above 5 sentences a thousand times. Write them with enthusiasm and write them as though you <u>really</u> want to believe.

I wonder why I think you CAN, and you think you can't? Because I know you are capable, smart and full of potential. I know this to be true. You forgot it somewhere along the way. Now it is your turn to think and believe it once more.

I remember a poster in a counselor's office. It said, "God Does Not Make Junk." Ever hear that? If you believe that God had something to do with making <u>you</u>, then you ought to think better of yourself, just knowing who helped create you. Right? You are special and it is time <u>you</u> think you are.

<u>You</u> have the ability to do wonderful things for yourself and for others. The time to start is <u>now</u>. Start this very moment to think well of yourself. You are worth it!

I wish <u>you</u> only the very best!

Doc

— — —

"The habit I have and would love to eliminate is that I am a stupid person. I won't amount to anything!"

Wow! That's quite a statement coming from a college student. You must have some <u>talent</u> and <u>potential</u> or you would not have been admitted to college. But, my telling you how smart you are is not going to solve your problem. <u>You</u> need a <u>new attitude</u>. I wonder how I can help you.

<u>You</u> need some reasons to think differently about yourself. Have you ever done anything well? Have you ever acted in a non-stupid manner? Have you ever done anything you can be proud of? Have you ever treated yourself with respect? Have you ever been kind, gentle, caring, loving, sharing, or helpful to someone else? I will bet that you have positive answers to each of these questions.

Ok, then, read each of the above questions and write down your answers, with pen and paper. <u>List</u> all the things you have done that you like, love and respect about yourself. Do not say you have none! You have many. You may just not want to recognize them. I want you to list <u>at least</u> fifty (50) items.

If you get stuck, ask the people who are closest to you for suggestions to add to your list. "What do you see that I have done well in my life? Have you ever seen me be nice to someone without being paid to do so? What have I ever done for someone else that made you proud of me? What evidence do you have that would prove I am not a stupid person? What do you think I ought to like, love or respect about me?" These are some examples of questions to ask your relatives, friends and peers in order to collect items for your list. You can say you are doing a research project for class and you need some feedback from friends.

You must have a "list" of items that convinced you you're "stupid," so now you need a list that proves you are <u>not</u>.

Our brains are like sponges. They soak up lies as well as facts. Our brains don't have filters to block out the untruths. It is possible to believe that Santa Claus flies through the air with reindeer on Christmas Eve; the Easter Bunny visits homes and leaves colored eggs; and we all came into this world with "original sin."

Once upon a time I was hired to teach algebra to 8th graders. Their principal said I didn't have to worry about teaching them algebra. He said the students in my classes had been failing math since first grade and were too dumb to learn. He told me to stay on task according to the Lesson Plan. I was given five classes and 163 "dumb 8th graders." They

187

turned out <u>not</u> to be "too dumb to learn math," they had just been taught that belief. It is possible to believe you are too dumb to learn math. If you had poorly trained or lazy teachers, then it is possible you didn't learn math, but that does not mean you are dumb. It means that you had poor teachers. You might have even been told by your teachers that, "You are dumb," but their feedback does not make it fact.

You have a "stupid attitude." You <u>think</u> you are stupid; therefore, you act like it. The fact is you aren't "stupid." You just <u>think</u> you are. Get it?

Now it's time to work on your, "I'm a bright, worthwhile, college student who can achieve good things in my life" attitude.

I have <u>never</u> thought of you as "stupid," and never will. It is simply not factual, and certainly not in <u>your</u> own best interest to think so. I believe that college is <u>DOABLE</u> for you.

Say this out-loud! "I can succeed at college. I can meet all its challenges. I have talent, potential, and I am worth the effort!!" Now, say it again, and again … and again.

I wish you success,

Doc

— — —

"I would like to change my attitude. When something goes wrong, or I get stressed, I tend to treat other people like garbage.

I agree with you. I think you ought to change your attitude. You do not always get what you want, neither do I. That's "life." So deal with your disappointments. I'll deal with mine. If you need some help, call on me, but don't treat me poorly in the process. That's not the way to earn my help and support.

When something goes wrong in <u>your</u> life, <u>you</u> treat others poorly? If you suffer, everyone around you suffers. I'll keep that in mind the next time you do poorly on a test in class. Ha!

Maybe you and I could make an agreement? You take care of <u>your</u> conflicts and I'll take care of mine. I'll handle my disappointments and will not share them with you. I am responsible enough, and mature enough, not to treat you "like garbage" just because I had a disappointment in my life. I'll bet you are just as capable. Besides, we all have both positive and negative events happen in our lives. We each get our share, whether we want them or not. That just seems to be the way life is.

Someone said, "If it doesn't kill me, it'll make me stronger." I seem to learn something each time life does not treat me as I want to be treated. I learn to cope better next time. Right? Conflict makes me more resilient. The more problems I solve, the more conflict I resolve, the better I am able to care for me. Critical thinking, strategic thinking, rational thinking and problem solving skills are invaluable tools for you and me. That's why they are part of a quality education.

It's bad enough to get less than you want, but there is no law that says you also have to whine and moan about your disappointment. I want all my students to attend class every session. Ten or fifteen percent are usually absent. Would it be appropriate for me to bitch at those in attendance because some are absent? Of course not! I decide to work with what I have. I work with who attends class. I don't moan and groan about those not in attendance.

Take what you get in life and do the best you can with what you get. The other option is to bitch, moan and groan because life gave you something different than what you wanted. Remember, your "bitching, moaning and groaning" makes you miserable. Who needs it! And, you're no fun to be around when you BMG!

I'm proud of you for recognizing your habit! I am also proud of you for wanting to change. Think about what I have suggested. If you need help, call on me. In the meantime, treat yourself and others with more respect. You deserve it. They will appreciate it too.

I wish you well!

Doc

— — —

"A habit I would like to get rid of completely is when I push people away when I am angry. I avoid confronting the problem and won't talk about what's bothering me."

While reading your concern, the first thought that popped into my mind was, "She must believe that she does <u>not</u> deserve the help and support of her family and friends!" Why would she shut herself off from others when she needs help the most? She must think that she is a bad person and deserves to suffer rather than resolve her issues and put them behind her.

So let's see. You cross the street and get hit by a car. You lie in the street both injured and angry. Help arrives, and you say, "Get out of here! Leave me alone! I deserve to lie here bleeding and alone!!" Is that what you would do? I sincerely doubt it. I think you would accept help.

How about a little different slant on the subject. You jaywalked. You are in the wrong. You get hit by a car. It was <u>your</u> fault. Now you are injured and angry at yourself because it was a "dumb" thing to jaywalk in the first place. Would you accept help now? I believe you would.

I think you would agree that you are a human being. As such, you are imperfect. You make mistakes, lots of them. We all do. When <u>you</u> make mistakes you also get angry. You make a mistake, and then you punish yourself even more by making yourself angry at yourself for making the mistake in the first place. Perhaps after you realize that you have made a mistake, you think you have not suffered <u>enough</u>, so you create some self-destructive anger to make matters worse? I strongly suggest you STOP punishing yourself anymore than absolutely necessary! You do NOT deserve it.

Did you know you have control over your anger? Did you know <u>your anger</u> is <u>your</u> anger? Yes indeed. You are in charge of what you upset yourself about, how intensely you feel the anger, how you look and sound when angry, and even how long you stay angry. It is <u>not</u> "The devil made me do it!" It is possible to make a mistake, even a foolish one, and not beat yourself up afterwards. It is possible to spill a glass of orange juice on your new blouse and <u>not</u> raise a big stink and push people around you away. Just wipe up the orange juice, change your blouse and move on. The damage has already been done. You don't deserve <u>more</u> punishment than that! Think about it. A mistake is a mistake. Even a BIG mistake is a mistake. Some folks I know spend entirely too much time "B.M.G'ing."

(bitching, moaning and groaning) over their shortcomings, rather than learning from them and moving on with their lives.

Recently I bought a very large jar of Bread-n-Butter Pickles at Costco. They looked so good I could not pass them up. I brought them home and opened them with my lunch. They were delicious. After lunch, as I was returning them to the refrigerator, the large, wet jar slipped out of my hands. The jar hit our kitchen tile floor with a crash. For a brief moment I was upset! Then, as quickly as the upset came, it went away. I reached for some paper towels and started cleaning up. It was no small job. There seemed to be pickle juice and pickle slices everywhere. I reminded myself that Costco had another jar waiting for my return. There was indeed life after a broken jar of pickles.

Now, had my wife been home, I would have gladly accepted her help to clean up the mess. You see, I had already lost my favorite jar of pickles and had a big mess to clean up. I didn't need to anger myself for long. I needed to clean up the mess. I didn't deserve the added self-abuse that anger would have provided.

Perhaps you need to say the very same thing to yourself. "This is already a mess. Getting angry and pushing others away is not required. It is not necessary. It serves no useful purpose. As long as I have a choice in the matter, I will spend my energy correcting the situation, if that's possible, and not use my energy to feel badly."

I like me. I like feeling good. When I think positively about life, I tend not to feel badly. I am a good person. I don't deserve to suffer. When I err, I will spend my energy learning from the situation rather than upsetting myself anymore.

A long time ago I wrote the following thought on the back of all my business cards. It is a statement that I made up and practice thinking. I still use it almost everyday of my life. As long as you are looking to change your habit of upsetting yourself, I will share it with you. *"I am too nice a person to upset myself without damn good reason!"*

You are welcome to use my thought as your own. I wish you well. Do feel free to call on me if you need some more ideas ... Doc

— — —

"I'd like to stop thinking that I need a drink everyday of my life!"

I assume you are talking about alcohol. I'd like to suggest that you see me for some personal advice about what to do with this issue. I think your concern is very valid, and I believe you need and deserve some help. Alcohol is not a subject to take lightly and I want to give you the finest help possible. I am very happy that <u>you</u> are concerned, and I want to take your request seriously.

See me, please.

Doc

~⊗~

ABOUT THE AUTHOR...

David A. Brown, Ph.D.

David has extensive educational preparation and professional experience in the fields of human behavior, counseling, innovations in education, program design and administration, and consultation and education. He has been a secondary school and university administrator; a college counselor and professor; the author, developer and director of grants for the United States Office of Education, the Office of Economic Opportunity, and E.S.E.A. Title III utilizing educational innovations; the director of comprehensive mental health centers; a counselor and consultant in Rational Emotive Behavioral Therapy; a school psychologist; and the director of operations for a Dislocated Workers Pilot Project with the Job Training Partnership Act. He has been the author and developer, as well as executive and clinical director, of an intensive, long-term, family-oriented, adolescent, drug rehabilitation treatment program in Florida. He has had more than 45 years of successes in encounters with drug abusers, would-be suicides, managers unable to cope, couples with marital problems, and juveniles with aberrant behavior problems. Dr. Brown has been a Professor of Psychology on the faculty at Hodges University (formerly International College) in Fort Myers, Florida for eighteen years. He retired in 2014.

He has developed and led successful experiential training programs in the Florida swamps to resolve interpersonal and intrapersonal relationship problems among high school students in high-risk areas for E.S.E.A. Title III. He has led groups of 300 pharmacists through personal conflict resolution experiences, as well as groups of neighborhood women and men in emotional survival encounters. Rational living, stress management, conflict resolution, and problem solving workshops were presented to industrial managers, school psychologists, college students, counselors and administrators, and J.T.P.A. participants with exciting success. Stress management, Rational Emotive Behavioral Therapy, and rational use of hypnosis are topics Dr. Brown has presented at numerous state and national conferences, service clubs, Chamber of Commerce, and other professional meetings.

He was board certified by the National Academy of Certified Clinical Mental Health Counselors, and the National Board for Certified Counselors, Inc. He earned certification in Rational Emotive Behavioral Therapy by the Rational Behavioral Therapy Center of the University of Kentucky, College of Medicine. He has served as Adjunct Instructor at Indiana University, Ball State University, Indiana Vocational-Technical College, and Edison Community College.

David is author of the books, The Pocket Therapist, The Pocket Therapist. II, and Anatomy of Attitudes, and has published numerous articles regarding the practical application of rational thinking.

He earned a Doctor of Philosophy Degree in Human Behavior from the United States International University in San Diego, California; a Master of Arts in Counseling from John Carroll University in Cleveland, Ohio; and a Bachelor of Science Degree in Mathematics and Education from Otterbein College in Westerville, Ohio. He completed intensive postdoctoral work at the Rational Behavior Therapy Center of the University of Kentucky, College of Medicine in Lexington, Kentucky, and at the Outward Bound School in Morganton, North Carolina.

Made in United States
Orlando, FL
15 November 2022

24576585R00115